PANACEA

CAITLIN SHELOR

Panacea

Copyright © 2020 Caitlin Shelor
Front and Back Cover Arts by Yvette Borja,
Trevor Shelor, and Mary Coastal Watkins
All rights reserved.
ISBN: 9798637592470

Dedication:

For Grandpy, who taught me how to grow and learn from pain. Thank you for everything. I'll never stop missing you.

1933 – 2016

Panacea:

a solution or curative to life's difficulties and diseases; coping mechanism; medicine

"Share your story with someone. You never know how one sentence of your life story could inspire someone to rewrite their own."

- Demi Lovato

Panacea

Panacea

Table of Contents:

	Image One	9
I.	Grandpy's Old Eulogy	11
	Image Two	15
II.	Inured to Body	17
	Image Three	37
III.	Atrophy of the Body and Mind	39
	Image Four	53
IV.	For My Sister	55
	Image Five	69
V.	To Granny (For Mom)	71
	Image Six	89
VI.	Death to My Youth	91
	Image Seven	111
VII.	Judgment	113
	Image Eight	127
VIII.	From Charleston to Parkland	129
	Image Nine	139
IX.	Grandpy's New Eulogy	141
	Image Ten	149
	Acknowledgments	151
	Image Eleven	159

Panacea

Panacea

Panacea

Grandpy's Eulogy

This is the eulogy I wrote for my Grandpy's funeral when I was fourteen. It has been slightly altered but is mostly the same.

Many memories can be made in a lifetime. Unfortunately, our old memories fall to the depths of our minds to be forgotten while other memories are made. Over the past few years, I'd forgotten many memories made with my Grandpy. A few weeks ago, while flipping through faded photo albums in search of the pictures I deemed worthy enough to include in a new album for the service, I found pictures from my childhood. My family and I flipped through pictures for hours, staying up past midnight, surrounded by clouds of decade-old dust. While my mom and my Aunt Debbie helped explain the stories behind the pictures, I began to remember some of them.

There were pictures of me with one of my absolute favorite toys: a big, plastic fire engine. It had two white front seats, a steering wheel, a grey overhead at the cab, lights on top, and a radio in the back, with a microphone to contact the "dispatch." Many months were spent with hair clinging to the overhead by static and hands swatting away at bugs in the back yard. Not to brag, but I was a pretty good firefighter, having stuffed animals as my crew; they lined the seats in the back of the firetruck, ready to depart when we approached the imaginary emergency. Grandpy bought that firetruck for me. He always had a great taste in gifts, like swing sets and bikes. Although, him being in my life was the greatest gift I ever received from him.

One particular memory that I am very fond of is when Grandpy read to me. Aunt Debbie explained this story to me with the most wonderful facial expressions I'd ever seen. Grandpy always hated the book *Chicken Little*, so much to the point that it physically pained him to even glance at the cover. But once, when I was a toddler, Aunt Debbie handed me the book and told me to take it to Grandpy for him to read it to me. So, I did, not thinking much of it since I was so young. He sat in this old reclining chair in the corner of the sunroom, and I waddled up onto his lap and asked him politely to read it to me. I gave him no choice, winning what I wanted with just my charming innocence, and he read it to me. When I'd gaze down at the page, he'd make faces at the adults in the room in a nauseated-looking way. But he read that book from cover to cover, and that is something I'll never forget. Not because of the faces he made, but because that was who he was: going the extra mile to make other people happy. He never wanted to disappoint anyone, especially me, and going through the pain of that book just to make a little girl happy is how I'll always remember him.

He was a fireball, always smirking and giving sarcastic comebacks that let him win almost every argument. Anytime we played cards, he would blow on the tips of his fingers and drag them across the table for good luck, insisting it was "a man's game." No matter how many times we attempted to convince him otherwise, he never gave up, even when I beat the pants off him at age ten.

As time goes on, things become less painful, so I must remember the best times. The inside jokes. From the stuffed rat to mixing up the colors blue and pink to those red pants he would never get rid of, even when they had a hole in them. The future will be rough, as it has been since Grandpy passed away. But Grandpy, knowing you're finally with Granny again makes everyone feel much better. Give her a hug for me. I love you.

Panacea

Panacea

Panacea

Panacea

Inured to Body

inured: becoming accustomed to something/someone unpleasant

I always felt there was something wrong with my body. Not the feeling that I experienced when I was eating dinner with my family or snacking on ice cream at Grandma's house at nine o'clock at night. It was the feeling I felt at my friend Jodie's birthday party, when everyone was running in the backyard, and this other girl, Annie, asked everyone if they wanted to race her. Annie had this beautiful blonde hair that fell to her waist and a smile that made boys forget girls had cooties, and she played soccer, so she was fast. Anyway, Annie and a few other girls lined up to race in Jodie's back yard, and Jodie said she would be the judge of who won the race. I decided to race, taking off my shoes, like everybody else, running over a pile of sticks and pine straw and dead leaves for nearly fifty yards, touching a tree, and racing back.

Once prompted, we all ran. I sprinted, leading the pack to the dilapidated maple tree in the corner of the yard, and tagged the tree first, a whole two seconds before Annie did. But as I ran back to the finish line, dodging the slower people who hadn't made it to the tree yet, my feet began to ache, sharp pains spreading from my toes to my heel with every step. I knew it was from the scratchy surface we were racing on, the mixture of sticks and pine straw and dead leaves that stabbed my feet every time they hit the ground. Figuring my feet were probably bleeding, I slowed my pace, attempting to take each step softer to ease the pain. In this, Annie caught up to me, and we crossed the finish line at the same time.

"Annie won!" Jodie shouted, hugging Annie, who shot me a cruel smirk that lingered on her face a little too long.

Looking down at my feet to examine the scratches and cuts, I mumbled, "We finished at the same time. If anyone was first, it was me."

Annie glared at me, and I knew her words would be filled with hatred and contempt, as if she forgot I was ahead of her for the majority of the race. "There is no way *you*," she looked me up and down, "could be faster than *me*." She looked herself up and down, admiring her own small figure.

"Guys, it was just a race," Jodie said, attempting to mediate, as if Annie and I were friends.

Deep down, I truly believed that, before the race, Annie told Jodie to say she won. Maybe she told her it would be funny, or maybe she threatened to not give her a birthday present. It angered me, but I grew self-conscious and embarrassed of everyone's stares, my cheeks hot and my stomach aching. They all looked at me the way she did, noticing the extra weight I had that none of them did. I wanted to cover myself, hide my body from everyone watching, feeling like a spectacle, a joke in front of these six first graders, especially Jodie, whose opinion I respected more than anyone else's. Luckily, Jodie's mother came out of the kitchen door onto the back patio and told us to come in for pizza, cake, and ice cream.

Everyone acted like nothing had happened as they sat around the kitchen table, eating too much pizza and leaving their crusts on their plates. Unlike everyone else, I only ate one slice, resisting the temptation to eat more. I wanted to look like Annie, so I could become Jodie's favorite and win races and not be the awkward chubby kid who ruins pictures and requires reassurance every time someone calls her "beautiful" for the rest of her life. So, I picked at the pizza and the cake and the ice cream, praying that it would soon be time to open gifts.

I don't remember what I gave Jodie. Maybe it was a stuffed animal or a board game or a Barbie. I just remember huddling on the far corner of the couch under a blanket, even though I wasn't cold, because I wanted to cover myself. I kept thinking about how everyone seemed so careless of their bodily contact with each other as they leaned around each other when Jodie opened her gifts. I was shameful of myself, of how my arms were touching my stomach when I placed them on my lap, of how I was growing breasts before everyone else already, of how I already had some slight stomach rolls. Parts of my skin touched other parts of my skin, and I anxiously grew sweaty under the blanket, though I refused to reveal my body to everyone else by removing it.

+ + +

A few months later, when I was in second grade, I made a new friend, Lydia. She invited me over to her house after school one day, and we walked there. In her backyard sat a nice swing set, with pristine new wood and a shiny plastic slide that captured my attention rather quickly. We played tag out back, ducking behind trees and the air conditioning unit and the trampoline.

I sat atop the slide, and, as Lydia climbed the steps of the playhouse, I slipped down the slide. Younger me thought this was hilarious at the time because I landed in the world's largest pile of dog poop. My friend felt terrible about it because she should've told me about the pile ahead of time, but I felt fine to just ignore it, maybe hose off my pants before getting into my dad's Jeep. But Lydia's father disagreed, insisting that he wash my pants. He mentioned that I could simply borrow a pair of Lydia's soccer shorts until my pants were clean. Lydia nearly burst into tears. The moment was no longer humorous to me.

"Daddy, can't she just wear her pants? Or a pair of yours, or Mommy's?" she pleaded, whining like I was stealing her favorite toy.

He shook his head. "It's just for an hour, maybe a little longer. What's the big deal?"

Lydia rose her voice again. "She'll stretch my soccer shorts out! She's way too big for them, and then they won't fit me anymore!"

I suddenly became aware of my size. To be honest, I wasn't even much bigger than her. She was like a twig, so thin that every bone in her body was visible, but I was slightly larger than average for a second grader. Perhaps I was a size Medium or Large in the kid's section in Target, while she was a Small. Even so, I didn't really see what the problem was, other than the fact that my new best friend had taken notice of my weight. She really thought it was important for me to be told how truly *fat* I was, as if I didn't already know. My stomach churned.

Lydia's father grimaced, grabbed his daughter's arm, and walked her inside, telling me he would be back out in a moment. I just stood there on her back patio, my poop-smeared Walmart jeans nearly falling off of me, as the poop weighed them down. Suddenly, my entire body was swelling. My stomach felt big, and my thighs felt big, and my chest felt big, and my reflection in the window of the back door showed a rounded face, rounder than the one I saw in the mirror that morning when I brushed my teeth before school. I wanted to pinch my fat so hard that it would just fall right off like barbecue ribs, the way it drops off of the bone with ease. I ran my fingers over my stomach and thighs in my reflection, tears brimming as my image distorted from how I thought I looked that morning.

As I refocused my gaze at the window, though, I peered into the kitchen and saw Lydia crying to her father while he squatted in front of her. At the time, I figured he was telling her that, yes, I would stretch out her shorts, and, yes, he would buy her a new pair, and, yes, he was very, very sorry. Looking back, though, he was probably telling her to get over it because it was just a ten-dollar pair of shorts. But it didn't really matter to me what he was saying, because she was crying, and it was all because I was the chubby friend who ate a little too much at meals and who was never signed up for sports until fifth grade basketball.

For the next hour and a half, I wore Lydia's shorts while my pants were cleaned, and I gave Lydia the shorts back before I went home, where I spent an hour staring at my mirror, my own glare tracing over every roll, every imperfection, every piece of excess fat that covered my body. I wondered why she was even friends with me if she hated how fat I was.

+   +   +

One of the only shows I ever saw with an "overweight" actress on it was *That's So Raven*, starring Raven Symone. A lot of people treated her equally until moments of racism and fat-shaming. It infuriated me how she was being mistreated for those reasons, since I didn't really think those were reasons to treat someone as less of a person. But this was one of the first, and one of the last, times I ever saw an overweight person on television as a central character. I thought she was aspirational, having good friends and wonderful talent despite not being a thin girl. And I thought she was beautiful. But there had been an episode centered around body image, and she was mistreated for her appearance, being told she didn't have the "right body type."

I sat in front of the television during this rerun, staring down at my seven-year-old body, how I wasn't thin either. After that, I couldn't ever find a show with an overweight character who was never mistreated for their weight.

Everyone was thin unless they wanted to be used for *not* being thin. It was typically a friend known for being the "overweight friend," and I came to the realization that *I* was the "overweight friend."

+   +   +

A year or so later, a boy who was with me, Jodie, and Lydia in the afterschool program suggested we play soccer over between the swings and the fence on the playground. A plastic, black boarder lined the perimeter of the swing area, and the fence that ran parallel to the swings ran along the perimeter of the kickball field. The fence and the boarder served as the two goals, and the space in the middle would be the field, despite it having no grass. I thought it seemed small, but maybe the bigger I was, the smaller those spaces felt.

Everyone who was playing actually played soccer outside of P.E., unlike me. I didn't really know the terminology or how to play much in general, so when Lydia asked me if I'd rather be the goalie, offense, or defense, I had no idea what answer to give her. I kicked at the rocks at my feet and waited for her to tell me what to do. Instead, the boy who proposed we play in the first place gave his opinion while exchanging looks with the two other boys who joined in to play.

"She should be goalie," he suggested about me, tucking the ball up under his small, fourth-grader arm. "She can cover a lot of space on the fence as a goalie."

Looking back, I can assume that maybe he meant that as a way of saying I was fast enough to run from one side of the goal to the other in time to block the ball, or that the fence was small, but in that moment, that wasn't what it felt like. I thought he was calling me fat, that I could take up a big part of the goal with just my overweight body, far more than any of my skinny teammates. In theory, that even made sense. But all I felt was shame as I looked to Jodie and Lydia for support. Neither one of them provided any.

Jodie nodded and opened her arms to catch the ball, which the boy had tossed to her. "Good call. I'll be defense. Lydia, you be offense. Girls versus boys."

This made the boy regret giving his input because now our team had a goalie who could block a lot of shots. I wasn't sure whether I should be proud that he wanted me as his goalie or embarrassed for the reason why. I never said anything, just took my spot at the goal and deflected as many shots as I could. This happened multiple times – us all playing soccer with me as the goalie, so many circular bruises on my legs from taking so many forceful direct hits, but it did occasionally make me feel important. Sometimes I hoped enough hits would knock the fat right off me, or it could break my leg and they'd have to give me surgery, where they could remove some of the fat while I was anesthetized.

+   +   +

In fourth grade, I tried to do something about it. I ate oranges during snack-time and only ate the healthy things in my stale school lunches of over-boiled corn and mushy carrots and semi-cold milk. My breakfasts consisted of a granola bar or an apple, so I could avoid Pop Tarts or muffins or bagels. I turned my favorite snack of half a peanut butter and jelly sandwich or some Cheez-Its into a cup of strawberry yogurt. Every day, when I woke up, I prayed to see someone else in the mirror. Someone thin and beautiful and happy, not someone whose body swelled like a sponge, no matter how many healthy things she ate and unhealthy things she didn't. Someone who could eat whatever they wanted and not need to exercise so much and still stay petite. Society has a view of beauty, and no part of my body could fit into their standards.

The summer after fourth grade, I attended a summer camp for a couple weeks. This one girl gave me disgusted looks every day of the camp. She was tall, and stunning, and at least three years older than me, and every day, when she caught a glance of me, she scrunched up her nose and rolled her eyes. Whenever I stood from a chair, she would sit on it or fold it up and slam it onto the clanking cart that held all the other brown, metal chairs. She would also talk whenever I did, but louder, like I wasn't even there.

Once, before it was time to eat lunch, I left the bathroom and drank water from the fountain on the wall outside. The girl left the bathroom as I stood at the fountain, and she purposefully shoved an elbow into me as she passed me, since she was so much taller than me. When I looked up at her, she whispered, "You should starve yourself," to me before turning on her heel and skipping back to the classroom. I couldn't believe nobody else was around to hear her say that to me, couldn't believe how correct she was. I was dumbfounded, staring at the water flowing out of the fountain into the drain. So, I wore an oversized jacket the next day.

+ + +

That feeling of being the chubby friend turned into my identity throughout elementary school, though. I knew that whenever other kids talked about me to each other and had to describe me, they always referred to me as "the fat blonde girl." Suddenly, I went from being an innocent little girl who danced alone in her bedroom to Taylor Swift and Justin Bieber to an insecure girl who flinched at the sight of mirrors and listened to sad Demi Lovato songs about bullying through a pair of eight-dollar headphones. Throughout elementary school, I remained friends with Jodie and Lydia, still avoiding Annie at all costs, but once I entered a different middle school than Jodie and Lydia, I realized that I needed friends that stuck up for me and were honest with me.

Though I discarded the old friends, the thoughts and memories remained, and so did the identity as the chubby girl, even until now, present day. I'm used to buying shirts two sizes larger than what my friends buy. I'm used to staring the opposite way when I pass reflective store windows. I'm used to growing sweaty faster than anyone else. I'm used to being tempted to cut off my fat with scissors. I'm used to jerking away at someone's touch because I fear they can feel how much more I weigh than them. Suddenly, I didn't require the insults of friends to cause me to feel fat; I could feel it all on my own. I think if I ever lost weight, I'd still be so used to covering every inch of my body, of not feeling like I lost enough. I always wish my hands were big enough to hide everything.

+ + +

Eventually, once I reached seventh grade, the amount I ate dwindled down, and so did my weight. Obviously, eating healthy and taking a two-mile walk every day was not helping, so I started packing less food into my green lunchbox that read "My Lunch" in hot pink lettering on the front. It lowered the number on the scale by about five pounds every one or two weeks, but when that plateaued, I removed my entire breakfast from my everyday diet on school days. It kept feeling like nothing would work until I finally stopped eating lunch, too, surviving off of whatever my parents made for dinner that night. Sometimes I felt unworthy of dinner, too, masking it with "I'm not hungry" or "I'm too nauseous to eat."

There was an event once when I spent the night at my friend's house for the first time. We were rough-housing, jumping around in her room and making jokes about our favorite dystopian novels. It was all fun until I bounced on her bed, and the cross-board under the mattress snapped in half. It clanked to the floor loud enough for her mother to enter the room in a panic. I assured her mother that I was fine, and I helped her collect the broken wood from under the bed, apologizing profusely for the mess, for breaking something. I knew the beds were old and rickety, and that it was bound to happen at some point, and all the other things her mother guaranteed to me in a calm, comforting voice. Even so, I felt ashamed, responsible for damage to something that wasn't mine. But more than that, I couldn't stop thinking about how I was so heavy I caused it to break. My friend had been sleeping on that bed for a long time without it breaking, but I fell onto it one time and snapped a board in half. Every step I took that night was so heavy as I tried to tiptoe with my overweight steps. My fat cheeks burned red hot for hours. I was a party pooper, but I couldn't possibly go back to the carefree feeling after I realized how heavy I was. This was something I knew I needed to take responsibility for, as it was my fault and nobody else's. Even my mattress at home was uneven from me weighing it down so much on one side. I knew I needed to make this change.

+ + +

People weren't even discussing my weight to my face anymore, but I didn't need them to in order for me to feel obese. I took pride in the gurgling vibrations radiating from my stomach, the acid crawling up into my esophagus, tearing away at the lining. It was painful at first, me clutching my belly and peering around for anything I could eat to make it stop, but once I grew used to it, I admired the feeling. It meant this system was working. I would sometimes even imagine that the stomach acid was scraping away at the fat from the inside and peeling it off layer by layer every single time I grew hungry. The constant hunger dissolved away my excess weight, and I loved it.

My parents hadn't noticed my weight-loss as much, how I dropped from a pant size twelve to a six in a couple of months. I definitely think one of the things that brought it to their attention was one time when I went over to my Aunt Debbie's house. As soon as I walked in the door, she smiled at me and poked my stomach. "Skinny," she called me, witnessing the change so clearly when she hadn't seen me in a month. It was rewarding, having me smiling as I strolled away with peach-pink cheeks. It sounded different than how I was usually told, "You need to do something about that tummy," or "I don't think you'll fit on the roller-coaster ride," or "we don't sell your size in our store." I wondered if my mom hung back in the doorway and confronted her sister about it.

I treated my habits like a diet. I could only eat healthy things, no snacks or treats throughout the day. It was rewarding – losing weight so fast. My confidence shot up as I no longer felt like the chubby kid. I was becoming comfortable in a swimsuit and in shorts. I didn't hate how I looked as much, aside from my braces. But then my dad noticed I wasn't taking lunch to school, and my mom noticed I wasn't paying for lunch at school either. One night, my mom confronted me about it, asking me if I was starving myself. I hadn't really thought of it that way, believing this was how I chose to diet; I associated an eating disorder with diet culture from this point forward. My mom assured me that this was not a diet, that as soon as I ate normal again I'd gain everything back and more, that other girls who did what I was doing ended up in the hospital or dead from malnutrition. I was put into therapy and forced to go back to three meals a day. I tried regular diets and exercise, none of which helped keep me small. It didn't erase urges. It didn't ease thoughts and desires to become less, to become smaller, to become new.

I often pictured this ultimate goal of how I wanted to look. It began as this girl with a slight muffin-top, enough to be cute but to still wear clothes that didn't show it. Curves that complimented every inch of her, like the up and down waves of a mountain. That idea then blossomed into a girl with a flat stomach, hard abs preventing her tummy from pooching out over her waistband. My final vision was a girl whose hip bones protruded further out than the stomach, which appeared to cave in. No fat. Just skin wallpapered up against the organs and ribcage and spine. Maybe I could be as thin as Lydia, never stretching out someone else's pants. Maybe I could beat Annie in a race. Maybe Jodie would stick up for me. Maybe I wouldn't break anything by just sitting on it.

Something I noticed with this anorexic eating disorder was that there was no such thing as "loosing enough weight" or "being the perfect size". I always wanted to lose more, even when I was only one-hundred-twenty-five pounds. But after being forced into therapy that didn't work when I was in eighth grade and having to fix my eating habits to a normal three-meals-a-day routine, the weight was quickly gained back with it, only more, like my mom told me it would. Pillow-like fat piled onto the exterior of my body in every possible place, thus diminishing my self-confidence and all the progress I'd felt like I'd made over the months where I wasn't eating. I cringe whenever my arm grazes against my body, whenever I generate far more sweat than anyone else, whenever I am touched by another person, even if it's as little as someone's fingers brushing against my back as they whisper, "excuse me," in passing.

I'm a hugger. I crave the intimacy of a hug quite often, of being held and comforted, but I worry that the person hugging me can feel stomach rolls and back rolls and jiggly fat and cottage cheese cellulite. As they feel it, they could visualize it, like being able to see me naked, and they could feel every pound of me, every drop of sweat, every stretch mark, every area of stubborn, unwanted body hair. Every imperfection. In a hug, someone can feel everything I hate about my body in one foul swoop. I've become selective of who is allowed to hug me.

Starting when I entered high school, I started eating what I wanted. Limiting myself to healthy foods never worked for me, even when I practically ended my sugar intake and focused on mostly organic and gluten free items at the grocery store. It changed nothing about my body type, so I was propelled into another type of eating disorder. The kind where I love food so much I almost obsess over it, so I grow even more obese. But on a dime, my mood changes, and I eat one meal in a day or make a fruit smoothie as my breakfast with no lunch. I turn down snacks and treats. I research liposuction costs, and I wonder, if I had a simple abdominal surgery, if they could cut my fat off while in there. This love-hate relationship sickens me every time I sit down for a meal. An eating disorder can be characterized by thoughts, as it does not have to rely on actions to be present.

I wish I could say this mentality disappeared as I ventured through high school. I wish I could say I've gotten better. But the mindset of this disorder never left me, despite what my actions may insinuate. I often contemplate returning to my old ways or wish that I could dismember parts of my body with scissors to trim off the weight, allow the mirror to show something less horrific. As someone who isn't grossed out by gory blood and organs, I envision a blade I could slice my stomach off with in one slash, quickly dropping forty pounds in doing so. Then I'd move to my thighs and hips, then my arms. I'd tear apart every flaw. The scars wouldn't bother me, because I'd weigh less. But I can't. So, I eat when I'm hungry, after enjoying the way my whole body vibrates when I've gone too long without food. I still walk with my chin a little higher when my stomach gurgles in hunger. This is not a cry for help – it's a daily struggle I deal with on my own. Some people are able to push past this mindset in their recovery, but I'm not sure if I can. I'll probably never be able to, either.

Panacea

Panacea

Panacea

Atrophy of the Body and Mind

The human body is one of the trickiest puzzles in existence, confusing everyone except its creator. As complex as it is, it fascinates me. Multiple organs working around the clock to prevent death: the one thing that is guaranteed. The puzzle of a body works almost perfectly, defending almost every cell. Almost. People die because bodies cannot always be protected from illness or harm. But I want to embrace and discover, as a surgeon, the puzzle of anatomy and save the lives of people whose bodies could not guard them.

A year before I was born, my Granny died from smoking, after years of having multiple heart problems, including a thoracic aneurysm. Her death left my Grandpy so depressed he didn't want to leave the ripped leather recliner in his living room for the next sixteen years.

Depression affects many parts of the brain, including the amygdala, thalamus, and hippocampus, which are all control centers for reactional response, thinking, and emotions. Loss of appetite, lack of care for oneself, irregular sleep patterns, inability to make decisions, physical and mental exhaustion, etc. My Grandpy was affected by each of those in his last couple of years. His health was rapidly declining. He knew it, too. I wish he cared.

When I was maybe six or seven, I used to visit him at his mountain house, and we would do everything together while my parents took care of my baby sister. It was as though my presence convinced him to interact with me, like he had to hide his depression from me. Sometimes we would go to a waterfall or an apple festival, then conclude the day with a puzzle or card game after my Aunt Debbie filled the house with the aroma of steak and baked potatoes that we ate for dinner; that was always his favorite meal. Sometimes I would have to teach him how to play a card game, like Slap Jack or Go Fish! And he would listen to me ramble on about the rules, then tell me I had a gift for helping people.

Sometimes, however, my Grandpy wouldn't want to leave the house. I always thought he was just being stubborn. Couldn't bring himself to go to the mailbox more than three times a week. His muscles atrophied, disintegrating and deteriorating beneath his skin. He couldn't build things with me anymore (one time we made a rocking chair together); or leave his recliner to eat dinner with us; or visit Costco to purchase abundances of books, movies, and food that weren't always necessary for his two-person household (he lived with Aunt Debbie). He couldn't get healthy, and he didn't really want to, either. And when he got diabetes, the only one surprised was him.

There was a day towards the end of March 2016 when my mom was supposed to pick me up from school, but when she texted me to ride the bus instead, I knew something was wrong. My mind began racing with multiple scenarios of what could have happened. The bus stop was right across the street from a small hospital that was not equipped for extravagant emergencies. I feared that maybe my dad was in a car accident, or my sister got sick at school, or my Grandpy was hurt. As I rode the bus to my stop, my stomach churned, my hands shaking and growing clammy. I knew it had to be something with my Grandpy.

My mom picked me up and began driving toward the hospital across the street. From the driver's seat, she smiled at me calmingly and told me there was no need to panic, but Grandpy fell. He was okay because Aunt Debbie was with him and had called 9-1-1. He had a brain bleed that was being absorbed back into the brain, so no surgery was needed, as it would only cause more problems.

At the hospital, each of my limbs shook as we waited to be escorted to the emergency room. The bland white walls hypnotized me as they sucked me back to his room, like they were washing me clean with antiseptic and pulling tears down my cheeks. He was lying in bed, television remote in hand as he ignored every word spewing from the doctors who had just brought him back from a CT scan. He smiled when I walked into the room, and he adjusted his position as if in an attempt to hide the bruise I knew was on his head. In all the years I spent with him, he never seemed like a particularly small man, but hospital beds and gowns seem to swallow people. They make even the largest people look little. Not weak, but small, fragile, vulnerable. Seeing him so uncomfortable caused bile to rise up my throat.

That night, when I got home, I stayed up until three in the morning doing research on brain bleeds, trying to figure out which kind he had, how long it would take to resolve, what could be done differently to help him achieve a healthier state in a shorter period of time. I believed that they should've done a craniotomy, removing a small portion of the skull in a surgery to access, assess, and stop the bleeding using only a microscope, some gauze, and forceps. That was an option, but my family took it off the table before I even knew what happened. Of course, brain surgery would have a long recovery time trapped in a white-walled hospital room, but he would be stuck like that anyway, as rehabilitation was needed. He could hardly walk. Apparently, he couldn't see when he fell, and since he had a brain bleed, he couldn't see much then, either. He needed rehab to survive, to walk across the room to the kitchen or bathroom, to drive to the grocery store, to balance out his blood sugar, to simply *breathe*.

He didn't want rehab, though. He didn't want to try.

The body often tries to match what the brain wants and needs. If the brain needed a break, the body would raise a white flag to surrender, crumbling into a sleep state so the body and brain could rest. Jumpstart like a car, charging like a battery, reviving itself like a defibrillator on a heart.

The entire family managed to convince Grandpy to go to a rehabilitation facility, as he needed to regain many functions again, like walking, since his muscles began to deteriorate. He slept all the time, lying in a worn-down hospital bed with a plastic television remote in his hand, controlling the channels he wasn't even watching, the volume he couldn't even hear.

When the body is preparing for death, sometimes the mind takes the person to a different place and time in their life, as if it is creating a bumper between the depressed mind and the realization of death, a distraction from reality as the time grows closer. This allows them to reflect on their life, to remember the most significant moments. Many people refer to this as "life flashing before their eyes."

In his last few days, he talked as if he was back in the Navy. Something about being on a ship somewhere in the Pacific. I remember one day when I was alone in the room with him, he mentioned needing to write, on Navy paper with a blue pen, a letter to Barbara (my Granny), which meant he thought he was back in Vietnam again. (A while later, as I helped Aunt Debbie clean out some things in the house, we found an entire box of letters he had written to Granny when he was in Vietnam.) It was as though he had Alzheimer's in the last couple days of his life. Another time, he thought he was talking to Granny, telling me he was excited about this wonderful house he found in the mountains – a getaway for them.

He clutched my hand in his and looked around at the empty room. "You'd love it, Dear. Especially in the fall. And there's a creek out back."

I nodded along to everything he said. Told him I couldn't wait to see it. And when it came time for me to go home, he said goodbye as though it was the last time. I wasn't sure if he still thought I was his wife or if he knew I was his first granddaughter. I still remember the feeling of his big hand clasped around my small one, giving one last squeeze before letting go.

My Grandpy fell into a coma on his last day. He was most likely audibly aware, but his reflexes, sight, and response were completely shut off, as though he was asleep. He was no longer the person I knew since birth, like he was hardly a person at all, just a body system. His skin was pale and calloused, wrinkled more than it seemed before, and his throat produced a death rattle often heard within the last few hours of someone's life. Sounded like he was gurgling water, breathing in a steady rhythm. It meant that the muscles in his throat relaxed, and secretions clogged the breathing, almost like snoring during a cold, or exhaling underwater. He was drowning in old age and lack of regard for his life anymore.

No doctor told us a distinct cause of death, other than age, as he was eighty-two at the time, only a little less than a month away from turning eighty-three. The brain bleed was ruled out, as the blood was still seeping into the brain as unhurriedly as possible. I was doing my own research, and my assumption was that, due to his diabetes and lack of nutrients, as well as immobility for an entire month (and however long he spent before then), many of his organ systems were shutting down, one at a time. He was probably septic. His respiratory system was slow to die out, still allowing him to breathe on his own by orders of the brain.

The brain was the last to shut down, cutting off the respiratory system, but the brain was slowly diminishing, control centers fading and failing. But, probably when he was in a coma, each of the other systems began to fail.

I remember my other aunt, Aunt Dawn, cupping my face and whispering to me, "You're the light of his life. He was so depressed before you came along, but you're his happiness."

Nodding, I cried, vowing to stay the entire night as he died.

The room was dark; the only noise, aside from the air conditioner, was the death rattle from his throat every two and a half seconds, keeping him alive. Another bed, which had been for a roommate he didn't have, faced the same wall as his, a curtain and six feet separating them. While listening to Grandpy's death rattle, I pulled out my computer to try to figure out if there was anything that could be done; there wasn't. I wondered if I could do CPR, if I could revive him myself, but I knew once his brain stopped trying, we would need to as well. During his last two hours, I fell asleep on the spare bed, half- awake in case something happened.

A mind can slip into a half-asleep mental state when certain conditions permit. Constant rhythm of noise or sound, such as music or someone speaking, could allow the brain to achieve this state. When constancy cuts off, the brain notices and awakens, alerted by the sudden change.

As I was sleeping, the death rattle was constant, and my mom talking to Aunt Debbie was constant. Aunt Debbie telling my mom that she was leaving the room to go home and shower did not wake me, as they had previously been talking. But, only a moment after she left, it was as though Grandpy heard her leave, heard the silence and felt he was alone. The sound of Aunt Debbie and my mom talking was constant for him, too, and the ended constancy allowed him to control one last thing, one last choice. His breathing slowed, no longer a loud rhythm. My mom was already calling Aunt Debbie, who only just reached her car in the parking lot, to rush back. The lack of constant talking woke me, tearing me from my dream of when Grandpy used to let me win at cards. He would blow air on the tips of his fingers, then drag his hand across the table for good luck before drawing a card, announcing, "I'm not gonna let you win this time," and I'd roll my eyes, then cross my fingers under the table, praying that he wouldn't get the card he wanted. Not letting him win meant he would try harder next time, that there would *be* a next time. But he won cards the very last time we played, and suddenly he was winning a chance to be with his wife again. I couldn't blame him for that, awarding his grave with roses every couple of months.

Some people, when in an adrenaline rush, lose all feeling and awareness of their bodies, a surge of nerves and energy seeming to block their nerve endings to prevent pain. For some reason, for me, in this instance, I felt everything. I was aware of every single movement, of every touch, of every cell in my body. This is part of the mystery of living that I wanted to solve, part of living that cannot be seen by a surgeon.

By the time I sat up and dropped my bare feet to the floor, stumbling over to his bed, he was breathing even slower. He exhaled between my steps. The first step I took, an image of him winning cards flashed by in my mind. Exhale. Step. Then him adjusting my hand when hammering a birdhouse to keep from hitting my finger. Exhale. Step. Him following Aunt Debbie and I around at a fish store while I searched for any fish from *Finding Nemo*. Exhale. Step. Him spending ten minutes pondering which book to buy himself at Costco when I'd already selected my own book eight minutes before. Step. Exhale. Him saying my sister had a pretty pink dress on and her correcting him, telling him it was blue and that he needed to go back to pre-school to learn his colors because she knew her colors and she was only four. Step. My eyes floated to his chest, waiting. (His shirt was white. He never mistook that color for another one.) No exhale. He stopped, and my mom fell into my arms, screaming. Aunt Debbie appeared in the door only seconds later.

I imagined watching someone's heart beating in their chest. A casual, steady eighty beats a minute. Feeding the entire body everything it needed to continue. Then it would stop, and perhaps I would know exactly what to do. Maybe I'd grab a defibrillator, or start chest compressions, or open up the chest. I'd be a doctor, and I'd save a life. There wasn't anything I could do for Grandpy, though. I was fourteen, and he wasn't here anymore to see me save someone's life one day. Checking the clock, I thought, *Time of death: 5:58am.*

"Did it just happen? Did I miss it?" Aunt Debbie asked.

My mom, who was sobbing, was in no position to answer the question, so I nodded.

"Are you sure?"

I nodded again. She fell into a chair beside him, crying as she held his hand, then stood and hugged my mom.

Everyone responds differently to traumatic shock. Some people become emotional and cry, some scream, some fall to the ground, some sit in silence, some deny, and some achieve more than just one of those. My mom screamed, then cried. Aunt Debbie denied, then fell, then cried. I was silent, supporting the weight of my mom as I stared at Grandpy's lifeless body, which looked remarkably similar to how it had for the years he spent in the recliner. For the next month after his passing, I could not sleep without the light on. Something about being in the same level of darkness as his room was when he passed made me associate the dim lighting with death. If a person is traumatized by a certain experience, their brain absorbs certain characteristics of that situation and associates them with the effects the experience had on them.

I don't know too much about medical terminology, so I am constantly learning, intrigued by the unknown. In that moment, I realized that perhaps a doctor could have saved him, and that nobody should be racked by the pain of loss. But he was ready. Life isn't just surviving or being fixed up by a surgeon, but rather the living done during the lifetime. This was his time to be done with the world, with its poetry, its laughter, its beauty, its hope, and its mystery. He always told me I had a gift for helping people. I want to help people in the future, people like him.

Panacea

Panacea

Panacea

Panacea

For My Sister

I remember the first time my sister asked me about same-sex couples. We were in my bedroom, sitting on the carpeted floor with the fan whirring above and a dim lamp in the corner illuminating the room in a soft yellow hue. She was in third grade, and she told me she saw two men holding hands in Target. The couple was shopping in the back by the candy aisle, like they were buying chocolate bars for a movie theater date. She wondered if they were normal, if they loved each other. The way she asked me about this, I knew my opinion would shape her own.

"Yes," I whispered. "They're just like everyone else. Some people only like women, some people only like men, and some people can like anybody. They can fall in love, just like Mom and Dad did."

She nodded slowly as she watched our cat enter the room, and she squinted in a way that said she didn't understand. "So, can a girl like a girl?" Her hand reached out to pet the cat, so she could have something else to focus on.

"Yeah. There's nothing wrong with it." I answered, nervous that she would then ask me if I liked girls. I took a breath to prepare for a question that, thankfully, did not come yet.

Deciding the best way to determine if my parents were against this part of me, prior to my coming out, I had the entire family watch a show called *Supergirl*, about this family that takes in a girl who has superpowers and is Superman's cousin. Her adoptive sister, Alex, once they've grown into adults in their upper twenties, comes out to the superhero sister, Kara. They share this beautiful scene in a place that reminds me of the Battery in Charleston, S.C., a park with a view of a vast body of water.

While the scene results in Alex announcing that she does not want to have the conversation anymore, it is still a very realistic portrayal of a girl who has fallen in love with another girl and decides that she should tell her sister about her feelings. Kara's confused expression as she sits on a bench facing Alex, who paces by the water, shows she is struggling to understand what this means for her sister, while still trying to be supportive. She later thanks Alex for coming out to her and treats Alex the same as she always did.

The importance of Alex's coming out is something straight people usually do not have to think of, as they never have to do something like that. This moment is monumental for Alex, as it is for any LGBTQ+ person who has to come out to their loved ones. Kara has a boyfriend nobody ever questions her about. She kisses her boyfriend ten times an episode, while Alex kisses her girlfriend once or twice, if that. I wish I could tell my sister that the affection on this show is not representative of their love for each other, but rather of how the television company chooses to portray them.

Sometimes I want to take my sister out on the dock in our neighborhood and sit on a bench with her, facing the water like how Alex did with Kara. I can imagine the river breeze tossing her short brown hair about on her head as she blinks quickly to keep her eyes from growing dry. She would probably be holding our dog in her arms because she loves physical affection, and I rarely give her any. Though she sometimes does not notice social cues from me, she would notice my anxiety, the way I'd refuse to say anything for a while until I'd eventually gather up the courage to take a breath and say, "I like girls." I'd hope she would take it as well as Kara did with Alex, or perhaps she would say what my mother said when I came out to her: "I already knew."

"It doesn't make me any different of a person than I already was," I'd tell her. "I'm still me." Maybe it would be this cliché moment, where we could embrace under the shadows of trees and passing birds as clouds part in the sky. Perched on the side of the dock, our feet hang, rocking back and forth. We smile to ourselves and stare out at the distance.

When Alex comes out on *Supergirl*, Kara asks Alex many questions, like how long she has known, and what all does this mean for her, and does the girl she likes like her back. If my sister were to ask me these questions, I would probably only answer the first one, telling her, "I have known since I was eleven, but I never knew how to tell you."

Living in a large city near an airport, an airplane would probably fly overhead, and we'd both look up at it, and she would be reminded that I'm moving out soon. "When you got off to college, will you get a girlfriend?" My sister, in my imagination, asks.

I nod and tell her, "Probably."

I'd lick my lips and taste the salty air drifting up from the river's breeze and picture a girl kissing me in the living room of an apartment I can only assume would be ours one day. It feels gentle and light, as delicate as the girl would be, and my arms would wrap around her enough to protect and comfort her. The girl smiles at me, hair tickling her cheeks before she tucks it behind her ear. Through a small laugh, she asks me if I want to dance, and I say yes, and we sway together in the kitchen.

In *Supergirl*, Alex grows tired of Kara asking her questions and says, "I don't want to talk about this anymore," then leaves the little bench area where she sat with her sister, concluding the scene. I imagine myself doing something similar, announcing to my sister that I am finished with the conversation and standing from the bench to walk down the dock again, back towards our house.

A day or two later, my sister would probably waltz into my room and ask me if I ever had a crush on a girl before. Depending on if I was busy or not, I would probably sit her down in my room and invite her into my own flashback from my childhood, a crush I only ever realized I had once I grew up.

Despite my silent vow of not joining the super girly games, I once snuck up to the clubhouse in the playground of my daycare and watched some of the girls play, "Bubblegum, Bubblegum," a game in which everyone sat in a circle with their feet together in the center. It was a counting game that I never won. I watched them from my perch, feeling as though I was gazing through a window or a one-way mirror. My five-year-old-self wishing I could sit elegantly and poised with a dress while surrounded by acorns and wood chips or laugh cutely like some of the girls could. Part of me believes I was jealous of the girls, and part of me believes I simply enjoyed being in their presences, wishing I fit in enough with them, that I could receive a second glance or thought. I wished they could see me the way I saw them.

One of my friends, Jodie, looked over at me, wearing a frilly pink dress and a bow the size of her head to match. "Oh, hi. Do you want to play with us?"

Nervously, I shook my head. "I don't really like that game."

She shrugged and turned back to everyone else, a few loose strands of hair framing her face. I wanted to climb up and move the hair out of her face, but my hands were too clammy, sticking to the bars of the ladder. My feet wobbled a little, so I climbed back down and fled to the swings.

A few years later, when my elementary school friends and I gathered around in a circle on my bedroom floor at one in the morning, they discussed who they had crushes on, and I felt left out, like I was in a neighborhood that wasn't mine. Normally, I would remain silent, and nobody would ever ask me, but one time my friend did. It was the same friend from the clubhouse, the one with the bow – Jodie.

"Is there a boy you like?" she asked.

Our other friends transferred their attention to me as I shook my head. "I don't like any of them. They're annoying."

Truth is, I strongly enjoyed being around Jodie more than I should have, mesmerized by her aura. *I think you're pretty*, I wanted to tell her. *I wish nobody else was here. Maybe I could be honest if nobody else was here.* None of my friends seemed to feel the same way I did: alone, secluded, unable to breathe steadily. I didn't know how to comprehend that feeling, so I stopped talking to her after a while.

My sister would probably continue to ask more questions after that, or perhaps she would stay quiet, figuring out which one of my friends it was. Only one of my old friends went to my preschool and my elementary school and had a bow. My sister can remember more than I give her credit for sometimes, able to recall the most random memories, like the time when Grandpy, Grandpa, and Dad built a playset for us in the backyard and didn't finish until sundown. She and I went outside through the clouds of gnats and mosquitos to run up the steps and tumble down the slide and rock on the swings for hours in the dark. We never grew tired, even with the calming cacophony of crickets and cicadas chirping in the hot South Carolina summer air.

Even though her memory is great sometimes, I wonder if she remembers a certain moment when we were watching *Supergirl* with my parents. The Alex character had not come out until the second season, so our family was hooked on the show by the time we found out about her homosexuality. We continued to watch the show, me smiling any time Alex and her girlfriend, Maggie, came across the screen. My Dad attempted to ignore the couple, talking about any other character, while I rambled on and on to my Mom and sister about how great it was to have minorities on television, how important it was for viewers to feel represented in a positive light, especially since Maggie is a Latina lesbian, which is even rarer to see represented on television.

In one scene, Alex and Maggie kissed, and my Dad quietly announced, "Do they have to kiss in *every* scene they're in?"

I glanced over at my mom, and she looked away, possibly disagreeing with his views but unable to voice her own.

"You say that as if Kara and her boyfriend haven't been making out this entire season," I retorted.

In that moment, I feared my mom suspected something since I took offense to it. I stayed silent, burying myself into the couch beneath blankets and pillows. My attention flickered over to my sister to see her response, as I feared, if she turned out to be part of the LGBTQ+ community like me, that she would be intimidated by his words and keep herself closeted like me. She was focused on the television, like nobody said a word.

Sometimes I wanted to hug the character, Alex, especially after that instance with my dad. I wanted to tell her I was sorry, that even though she helped me gain confidence, I still couldn't come out. Not yet, at least. I also wanted to feel close to her, feel the warmth of her female body pressed against mine, the closeness of knowing I didn't have to pretend with her. She was out and proud, and I wanted to be, too. And I want to be out to my sister, the way Alex is out to hers.

Part of my fear about coming out to my sister isn't even about her, but rather how my parents would feel about her knowing. It almost feels as though I have shoved my sister into a closet because I have refused to tell her anything, avoiding questions and fussing for her to leave my room. We're suddenly both in closets facing each other's closed doors.

Sometimes I picture my mother saying something that Simon's mother said in the movie *Love, Simon*. Simon had just come out to his parents, and he was struggling to cope with the aftermath of being "outed" at his school when his mother gave some comforting words of wisdom: "You are still you, Simon. […] You get to exhale now, Simon. You get to be more *you* than you've been in… in a very long time." This should be freeing.

Attending an arts high school has given me a lot of freedom with expression of my sexuality, allowing me to feel as though I can be open without judgment. In fact, I only really came out once or twice with people at my school because it has become so normalized that I sometimes don't even feel like I need to come out to people there. But I remember the first time I said my sexuality aloud.

I walked out onto the sidewalk off campus where my mom normally picked me up. I had yet to close my jacket, as I was wearing a shirt I had painted a rainbow onto with "Love is Love" etched onto the cloth in Sharpie. Another rainbow was smeared onto my face with makeup. I wore a hoodie in the car with my dad to ensure he wouldn't see the shirt, but I peeled it off when I got on the bus that morning. While I waited for my mom to pick me up, a girl from my school walked up to me with her friend. She wore a colorful, tie-dye shirt and a rainbow tutu with high-heels to perfect the entire look. Her friend's outfit was similar, except he was a guy. He, too, wore a tie-dye shirt, but his pants were striped and multicolor. Their attires made me smile.

The girl said to me, "I like your shirt."

I nodded in response. "I like yours, too. Well, your whole outfit. Both of yours." I gestured to each of the students, suddenly unable to speak.

She laughed. "Thanks. Are you gay?" This wasn't to be invasive but simply to see if I was an ally or a member of the team, as some people say. It was a question I was unprepared for, but it wasn't an uncomfortable question, either. After the rainbows marching down the halls and the "GAY OKAY" chants at lunch, it was a normal thing to ask.

"I'm pan. Are you?" My nerves began to fall away, as I was suddenly being honest with a stranger. The words felt new on my tongue, yet also satisfying.

Her eyes grew wide and her smile floated up her face to her cheeks. "No way. Me, too! And so is he." She pointed to her friend, who nodded and laughed; he didn't seem to be fazed by her announcing his sexual orientation, like she had simply stated that he had pink hair (which he did). I wondered if it meant he was proud. "Well, have a nice day! See you around."

I mumbled the same to both of them and watched them skip down the sidewalk, how they purposely crunched dead, fallen leaves under their shoes and laughed about it. Carefree.

This moment is important to me. It reminds me of a scene on *Supergirl* when Alex parades around a bar telling everyone there that she had a girlfriend, because she was ready to be open to the whole world, having nothing to hide. I wanted this to be me. That's why I write this. For my sister. For my family. For everyone who chooses to read it. I want my sister to know that I am not ashamed of my humanity. My attraction to other humans is based on personality, not gender. I have no reason to hide this from her because my parents already know, and my sister does not view it as a negative aspect a person can have. She's an accepting person, as I always hoped she would be.

Panacea

Panacea

Panacea

Panacea

Panacea

To Granny

(for Mom)

I don't know how old I was the first time my mother told me about you. It feels like I always knew about you, even when I needed to be reminded when I was four or five of who you are. We were eating dinner in Aunt Debbie's kitchen – me, my mom, Aunt Debbie, and Grandpy, and Aunt Dawn might've been there, too, and I think my Daddy was home with my baby sister – and someone made a reference to you, calling you Granny. I was confused, never really thinking I had more than one grandmother, so I asked who you were. All I can really remember is the low lighting and disturbing silence that immediately followed my question. Just wind blowing outside the windows, and Aunt Debbie's dog's collar jingling under the table, and Grandpy still eating what was left on his plate, utensils clinking. Nobody knew what to say.

Her face grew red as her eyes collected tears, and she smiled, touching her wine glass lightly to give her hands something to do. "Granny was my mom, your grandma on my side of the family. We call her Granny."

At first, I just imagined an older woman, a head full of thin grey hair, hovering over a cane and adding an extra syllable to every word the way older women do. But then I pictured an older version of my mom and my aunts, all their faces combined as one. Short, maybe a little rounder, like the rest of our family, and I wondered if you wore pants and a t-shirt like me and Aunt Debbie did or if you wore a fancy blouse and skirt and pearls like my Grandma. Even in every possible image in my head, you had thin, nimble fingers. All the women on your side of the family had tiny hands – that's where I got mine from; my mom still wears a size four or five in rings. My dad said he would've saved a lot of money if he had just bought her a kid's ring, rather than gold and diamonds. He was just kidding.

"Can I meet her?" I recall asking, hands tucked under my thighs as I swung my legs under the table, eager.

More silence sunk in at this request, everyone exchanging looks. I can remember everyone's questioning facial expressions, except for Grandpy's. I'd like to think he smiled at this, but maybe he was near tears, or maybe his hearing had already started to go at that point and he hadn't heard the conversation, too focused on when the apple pie in the oven would be ready or watching his dog roll around on the floor with Aunt Debbie's new dog, or maybe he was suffering from a blank stare at his reflection on the window of the French doors to the porch that sat about five feet behind where I was at the table. Perhaps I can't remember how he looked right then because my own memories of his face have begun to fade since he died a few years ago.

"Honey…" my mom whispered as her hand left her wine glass to caress my arm. "Granny died before you were born."

I distantly remembered a time when we had gone to a cemetery on Christmas or Mother's Day or Easter. It was almost always raining, so the air was muggy and prevented us from ever staying long. My mom would stand over the headstone and just stare at it, and my dad would rub her back. Seeing tears brimming my mom's eyes, I would hug her leg or hold her hand. But I never knew what to look at, so I'd always kick softly at the dirt and watch as the ants crawled around me. My dad glared at me when I stomped on the ants. These minor memories helped me place your death together with the grave at the cemetery. For all I know, my mom could've told me sooner about you, but my childish mind could have forgotten by then.

In that moment, I wondered what motherly instincts my mother got from you. When I used to try to climb over the back of the couch, my mom would always fuss at me, and I wonder if you ever fussed at her for pretending the world was her jungle gym. When my mom used to allow me to stir cake batter but never pour anything or crack eggs, I wondered if you would have made the same rules. If you had taught me to cook, would you have gotten mad at me for spilling flour or falling off the back of the chair? Would it have been an "I told you so?" Would you have whispered a secret to me, telling me that Grandpy slept with his mouth open, and I could see it from the kitchen if I peeked around the counter into the living room. Maybe you would've informed me that adding a dash of nutmeg could improve an entire dessert dish if given in small doses, and you would've guided my hands when pouring it. Would I have been more obedient around you than around my mom, like I am with my Grandma? Would your voice make me shiver when I was in trouble? What other traits did you pass down to the women of this family?

"Why?" I asked, the way kids always want to know *why* something happened or *why* something is the way it is.

She seemed to think for a minute, like she didn't know how to answer. "She was... sick. She got really sick before she died."

"Was she nice?" I so badly wanted to go back in time and meet you.

Aunt Debbie nodded. "She was. And funny. She was a *hoot*! You would've loved her."

I know I would've. I think I even do. But having never truly met you, maybe I only love the idea of you, never knowing what made you laugh or cry or yell or smile. To me, you're a mythical creature, an untouchable woman with power and love and beauty. Maybe I only love the idea of having *two* grandmothers to spoil me and teach me things like baking pies and tying my shoes and crafting a present for my mom's birthday. Maybe I only love the things you did for my mom and aunts and Grandpy, making them happy and encouraging them to keep living, even after you'd passed. Maybe I only love the women you shaped your daughters to become – gorgeous, caring, compassionate, brave, powerful, enough humor to fill a quiet room for hours. I tried to imagine you laughing, but at that time, I hadn't seen any pictures of you, so it remained the image of all your daughters' faces blended together into one.

Aunt Debbie recently described a memory of you to me. She said you two and the rest of the family went up to

Maggie Valley, staying in a rented mountain house on an annual week-long trip. This house had a creek out back, with a fallen tree passing over it, dead. A yellow rope hung above, dangling from a tree to pose as a handle to let people cross. Aunt Debbie, a young girl at the time, clasped her hands around the rope, peeking over her shoulder at you as she motioned you closer, hopeful you'd join her.

"Come across the tree with me," she begged you, grinning and dancing a little beside the tree as encouragement.

I imagined you smiling and shaking your head, refusing to let your feet leave the firm ground. You probably didn't want to get your pants wet from where the ground was muddy.

"Come on, please? It's easy. Look!" Aunt Debbie grinned as she started over the tree, still clutching the rope.

She went back and forth several times in efforts to prove the sturdiness of this tree to you. I thought of the scene in *Bridge to Terabithia* where Jesse and Leslie repeatedly crossed the creek with a rope, swinging back and forth like Tarzan. I wondered if I could have convinced you to cross it with me. I imagined you rolling your eyes as she made each of these trips until you would've probably widened your eyes at the sight of Aunt Debbie's foot missing a step on the tree, causing her to slip and fall into the water. She sat there, frightened and soaked and embarrassed, and back up on the bank, you allowed your pants to get dirty when you laughed so hard it put you on the ground. You could hardly see your daughter for the laughing tears obstructing your view. Mud seeped into your pants, probably staining them, but you didn't care because this was so funny to you, how karma worked itself out. Aunt Debbie slowly lifted herself out of the water, dripping puddles everywhere as she struggled to escape the creek. And you just kept laughing. Aunt Debbie was right; you *were* a "hoot." I wonder how much you'd laugh at the pathetically hilarious jokes I tell. I wish I could laugh with you. Does your laugh sound like my Mom's, or mine – another trait passed down through us women?

When I was three or four, my daycare went on field trips on every Tuesday over the summer to the pool in Melrose, the neighborhood you raised your children in. My daycare didn't have a bus, so we all piled into the owners' and chaperones' cars, sitting in our booster seats that put us barely tall enough to see out the window. Sometimes my mom would chaperone, and I remember watching out her window and seeing your house, which Aunt Debbie owned and lived in by then. I'd never gone past Aunt Debbie's house before, but then I started to learn the way to the pool.

I was too young to be allowed to just jump into the pool, so my mom had to stand in the water and catch me when I jumped. She helped teach me how to swim and jump, watching me flail about in the air before plopping into the water just a few inches from her face. Whenever I slipped beneath the water, my mouth forming bubbles in front of my face, she scooped me up, apologized for not keeping me up. Maybe I should have apologized for splashing her in the face, rather than giggling about the water she had to cough out of her mouth. She told me about how she used to swim in this pool every day, rain or shine, cold or hot. She grew up in this pool, the way I grew up in my Grandma's pool. She was on the swim team, and looking back, I wonder if you taught her the way she taught me: gentle love. Slowly easing her into learning to stay afloat. Or did you send her tough love, leaving her thrashing about in the water until she discovered how to find the surface? Would you have taught me to swim the same way you taught her?

Memories like this makes me wonder what else you could've taught me. Mostly about being a woman. What it means to be independent. Aunt Debbie told me that the most important thing you ever taught her was to never ask a man to do what you can do yourself, to learn from other people so you can do it on your own in the future, to let everyone in the room know you have just as much to say as they do and that you can do whatever they can – only better.

But this wouldn't have been taught by sitting at the kitchen table and having a "girl talk." You would've shown her. She said that's what you'd do. You showed people how to do things, let them witness your greatness in action. I try to imagine how you'd go about teaching her that, or teaching me that. Perhaps I would've asked my dad to do something, and you would've shaken your head at me and told me that you knew how to do it and could show me. Would you have forced me into dresses when I pleaded to wear nice pants and a shirt? Could we have avoided going clothes shopping? Would you have shown me how to do more than just the stereotypical female duties, like cooking and planting flowers and folding laundry? Would you have taught me how to make sure I'm financially stable enough to be on my own, if I must be at some point? Would you have taught me how to know when you're in love, or how to propose to *the one*? Would you teach me how to fix something on my car? Would you have gone to the Women's March with me? Would you be proud of the feminist I am today?

You used to wear makeup and perfume, and I wonder if you would've tried to teach me how to do my makeup. Would you have used a new makeup company after hearing about animal cruelty charges or a racist C.E.O.? I don't know if you teaching me the proper way to blend or shade would've made me care more about my appearance and want to wear makeup all the time. Maybe I would've just told you that I didn't care about makeup and never put it on again. Sometimes I seek to please people too much, my own feelings often left behind in the stretch to elicit smiles. Almost gratification. See, that's the thing about women – we're taught to politely grant other people's wishes, but the most important thing when growing up is realizing we don't have to unless *we* want to.

I'd like to think you are a feminist. I want to know everything you hated and everything you loved and everything you stood for. Everyone always says you were the type to never let a man do what you can do yourself, unless you didn't have enough hands or were running out of time, in which case I assume you would gladly accept help. But would the believing in the power of a woman just end at a white woman, or would you have stood by that belief for all women everywhere, black and white, cis and transgender, old and young, every color and gender and age in between? Would you fight for the rights of people you've never met?

Aunt Debbie told me of a time in the 90's when the woman who cleaned your house stole your ring. I imagine you thought it was funny that someone would steal a ring from someone whose ring size was obviously too small for the average woman. There's no way it could've fit that woman's fingers, leaving her sitting there trying to shove it on a fat finger in her car before realizing her finger would not shrink, so she would've had to try to profit from it by giving it to someone. That's why you had a hunch that you could possibly find it. You called the police to report this theft and wasted no time trying to find where the ring had been taken. While your husband insisted you wait for him to return home, you continued to search for this ring until you found it at a shady pawn shop on Rivers Avenue, where you and a police officer fought to get the ring back. I imagine you standing in a pawn shop, hands on your hips as you stared into a glass case at the row of gold wedding rings until you found yours, where you probably would've pursed your lips before you unloaded your anger at the man behind the counter to get your way. The police officer probably just stared at you, watching you take complete control of the situation. You won and got it back, and you didn't have to wait for your Navy husband to come home and do it for you.

After hearing this story about you, I just know that you were no ordinary housewife. No, you were a feminist, a powerful woman who did not wait at home for a man to do a job she could do on her own. And if you ever did something that seemed like you were accepting a stereotypically sexist act toward yourself, you were actually using it to your advantage, knowing exactly how to fold a man around your fingers. The basic 1950's white man agenda proved only as an obstacle to you, yet you manipulated it to work in your favor in the most graceful way. And I just know we would have been close because I strive to be as confidently independent as you.

Working as a secretary for most of your life, I have to wonder what the worst or most obnoxious thing you ever saw was, your job designed to assist the men around you. How did you navigate sexism? How did you make your voice heard when men approached your desk claiming to know more than you? Claiming to be *smarter*. Claiming that you were *inferior* to them. I wonder if it ever irritated you to have someone hold a door for you or flirt with you to get on your good side. Did you ignore it? Did you use it to your advantage?

If you walked into the room right now, as our first time meeting, I wouldn't know what to say to you. Would I have to introduce myself, or would you recognize me? I'm not sure I'd recognize you, as I still sometimes try to merge all your daughters' faces together when I attempt to envision you, though I have seen real photographs of you.

I imagine you entering my safe place – the house in Maggie Valley. You'd knock on the door, and I'd reluctantly open it, assuming you were a neighbor. Nobody else is home in this visualized scene, so I just stand there, door wide open, welcoming. The chilling springtime breeze would waft into the room to the sound of birds chirping and leaves brushing against each other, and it would almost feel like a sign of who you are. It's odd to think that you've never even been to this house before.

"Granny," I whisper, unsure if it's a greeting or a question.

You'd nod, probably smile. "I see your Grandpy taught you to call me that." It sounds like it's something you never wanted to be called until I was the one to say it.

I imagine us sitting on the front porch of the house, each in a rocking chair with a cup of coffee in our hands. I never drink from mine, allowing it to grow cold in the cool mountain temperature. The sun peeks behind the trees and paints the lawn and our pale skins in a light hue, splashing us with butter, such a sweet feeling. Above us, a hummingbird hovers beside the feeder, never once landing as it drinks from the red sugar water. A small gust blows again, your short hair flittering a little.

You don't say anything, just look down at your coffee.

I squint in the sun, catching short glimpses at you. "How's Grandpy?"

You give a satisfied smile, but then it falters. "He's okay. But I think he regrets not staying to see you grow up."

I give you a questioning look because when he was here, all he wanted was to be with you, so why should he be anything less than happy? "He does?"

You look up and tilt your head a little, nodding. "Yes."

It is evident that you regret every cigarette that made you so sick that my mom didn't want her baby to only remember you as the sick grandmother. You were so ill. My mom wanted to protect me, the way us women protect each other. I understand why. I would've done the same thing. I can see that you wish you tried to change your life before it was too late. You know I see this. So we just sit here for a moment. More birds chirp from the trees across the street, and a child giggles in the distance. The sunlight soaks us in a honey glow, slipping in and out through the dancing trees and cumulus clouds, like cotton. Anxiety washes off of our bodies in the drips from the sun, so comforting for two strangers to share this moment together. Purifying.

You sip from your coffee, then look over at me. "You don't drink coffee, do you?"

A smile creeps onto my face, and I shake my head. "I don't like tea, either. No caffeine for me." This is when I realize there is so much you don't know about me, things that I never even had the chance to tell Grandpy before he passed away. So many things I was too scared to say. So many things I didn't know about myself until after he was gone.

"Migraines?" you ask, and I nod. "Aunt Debbie gets those, too."

I suddenly gain the urge to inform you of so much. "I'm a writer, you know. And a photographer. I have Grandpy's old cameras."

"Oh, really?" you grin, eyebrows raised as if you didn't already know this. "That's amazing."

I'd like to think you'd be proud of me for other things. For the person I've become, for who I want to be, for what I've accomplished. Maybe you would've come to every single recital, every basketball game, every writing reading, every Honor Roll award ceremony. Maybe I would've become a different person. But maybe I wouldn't be who I am. Maybe I needed to never meet you, so I could feel loss and absence so young, so I could be a writer, so I could grow.

I nod, tracing an edge of the wooden porch with my fingertip to chase an ant away from my leg. "Did you teach my mom and aunts how to ride a bike?"

You're taken aback by this question. "What?"

"Grandpy helped teach me how to ride a tricycle, and he bought me several of my bikes over the years. Who taught my mom and Aunt Debbie and Aunt Dawn?" I recall a photograph I've seen of Grandpy pushing me on a tricycle when I was two or three.

"Your Grandpy taught them. I watched." You force out a small laugh from between your lips as you look out at the yard, spotting butterflies on the flowers.

You're distant. Having worked around Navy men, you were forced to be tough. But just by looking at you, I see that you had those men around your small finger. You were in charge of everything, and you knew it – a powerful woman. Those men could never bully you into anything. I admire that. But I want you to be softer with me. I want you to tell me why Dalmatian dogs are your favorite. I want you to tell me you want to teach me how to cook your favorite meal, perhaps meatloaf or chili or something I've never heard of (and trust me with knowledge of the secret ingredient or way of mixing). I want you to tell me where your favorite place in the world is – maybe Japan because the cherry blossom flowers are beautiful there. I want you to tell me what you think the worst movie is. I want you to tell me if you want to meet all my friends, the way my Grandma does. I want you to see Aunt Debbie and Tony get married. I want you to tell me you can't wait to see me get married. I want to ask you how you'd feel about me marrying a woman. But I can't ask about those things. At least not the last one. I can't imagine your reply. I can't imagine you telling me if you'd still love me or not. I'd like to think you'd hold me tight and ask me how my wedding would look, if I'd want to wear a dress, what color flowers I'd want on the tables. Maybe you could ask me what things would make me fall in love, if I knew the age I'd start to consider getting married, if I wanted kids. Maybe I wouldn't even have to convince you that I could still have a family with a woman. Maybe it wouldn't change anything.

I watch a chipmunk burrow into a ditch with a baby on its back. The children who giggled earlier zoom past us on their bikes – two girls, like me and my sister. Despite not knowing if you like physical affection or not, I wrap my hand around your arm and rest my head on your shoulder, confident that you'd love me, not caring how different I am than whatever you imagined your granddaughter to be. I know it deep down that you know everything I want to tell you, but my idea of you only lives through what other people have told me, so I only keep imagining us like this, conversing about love and heartbreak and jokes that have us gasping between laughs, just two women on a dusty porch – perfectly still, but rarely silent.

Panacea

Panacea

Panacea

Death to my Youth

- Virginia Tech, April 16, 2007 -

One time in elementary school, my school let us dress up for Halloween. I don't remember what I was, but it was second grade, and I remember several boys wore police officer costumes. With their plastic batons thumping against their legs and cloth hats blowing off in the wind, they ran around on the playground putting plastic handcuffs on pirates and princesses and bumble-bees. Some of the police-officer-boys complained about not being allowed to have fake pistols or Tasers on their costume's belt. Nobody our age really seemed to understand why the rule was what it was; Columbine was before our time, but we were never told about it. In those days, our parents kept us so sheltered that we didn't even really know what a school shooter was.

The first main school shooting of my time was the one at Virginia Tech. My parents never told me about it when it happened. Never told me about the thirty-three students and teachers that were killed. Never told me about the seventeen people that were lucky to survive their bullet injuries. Never told me about the numerous people injured attempting to escape, to save their own lives amidst the rapid gunfire.

A couple months after that shooting occurred, a little while into the new school year, our principal had everyone participate in a Code Red Drill, where we sat in a corner of the classroom hidden from windows and doors and waited quietly until the principal announced over the intercom that we could go back to normal activities. After the announcement, everyone was called into a major meeting in the gymnasium. We were instructed to silently sit in rows with our class, organized by grade, on the glossed-over, maple-wood floor while listening to a presentation.

I never really learned much about the Virginia Tech shooting until I visited the school with my Grandpa, who was an alumnus. It was a beautiful day, with the sun cascading over the trees so softly I could see the pollen particles floating down like yellow mist. The grass glowed a vibrant green in a field across from a memorial. Nobody ever told me how many victims there were, but when I saw a semi-circle of large stones beside some shrubs near the sidewalk, I was shocked by the number of stones there were. I started at one end of the semi-circle, squatting down to sniff the flowers at each one as a I read the names.

"There's so many," I whispered, and my Grandpa nodded.

"Thirty-three," he read from the plaque that stood in the center of the semi-circle.

This seemed like something I should have known many years ago, as no tragedy should be forgotten. As I look back, I am grateful for the way the principal refrained from telling us the real reason why we had this meeting. My six-year-old self was not ready to learn about school shooters. But nobody is really ever *ready* to learn about them. A few years later, many six-year-olds were forced to learn about school shooters in the worst way possible.

- Sandy Hook, December 14, 2012 -

I always thought it was fun to play the quiet game during Code Red Drills. Everyone sat all hushed in a corner that was invisible to all the windows and doors, legs to chest, whispering to the person huddled beside them while the teacher promised candy to whoever didn't talk the entire time. The two fastest kids hid beneath the teacher's desk, and it always made them the coolest ones in the room because they had a cover over their head, a little hideout.

It wasn't until the Sandy Hook Elementary School shooting, when I was in fifth grade, that people really started to understand what the Code Red Drill was really about. All the schools in the district suddenly had a new rule: don't actually listen to the administrator who says we're free to resume class-time. The administrator would come over the intercoms and say, "Alright, everyone. The drill is over, and you may now resume normal classroom activities." We were instructed to stay put, to keep quiet and leave the lights off, to not scream if we hear someone in the hallway. Then, someone would come around, fist pounding on the door while jiggling the handle that was supposed to be locked. If the door was locked, he would continue onto the next room until he went to every single room, which took about thirty minutes. If the door was unlocked, he would come in and point his finger at as many students as he could see, then say, "You're all dead." He would look at the teacher, eyes narrowed as if to say, "You just killed all of these children." The S.R.O. came around to unlock each room, and that was the *official* sign that we could resume normal activities. If we had gone to our seats when the administrator told us to over the intercom, the locked door wouldn't have mattered because the "shooter" would've killed us through the window in the door.

I remember asking my teacher that year a question that puzzled her: "What if a bad guy came in and shot the people at the desk and took their keys and unlocked all the doors and shot everyone in the classrooms?"

Her nose twitched, like she wanted to tell me not to say something so dark in front of this classroom of ten- and eleven-year-olds. "I don't think that would ever happen."

"If they came and shot the desk people, who would tell us to hide?" someone else piped up from the back of the room.

"Well, I think you would hear the gunshot," another kid stated with an impolite attitude. He was the son of a hunter, so he would know what a gunshot sounded like.

The teacher attempted to quiet everyone down, as everyone was asking questions all at once, but it didn't work. It was chaos – everyone realizing we could all be killed so easily at such a young, vulnerable age. Everyone was scared. Their volume increased my anxiety, so I eventually quieted everyone down with my next question.

"The bricks are bulletproofed, but if a door opens, it doesn't matter, right? My dad says it makes us sitting ducks. Why can't we just run?" My proposal demanded a lot of attention and support from the other students. So much for keeping the classroom under control.

A girl, who always seemed relatively inaudible, rose her voice for the first time all week. "I'd rather try to run away than be trapped in this room, waiting for a bad guy to find me."

The class clown weighed his opinion next. "I'd fight 'em. Why let 'em go on to the next room after he found this one empty when we can take 'em out? One guy versus thirty-two kids and a teacher? We'd totally win." He flipped his hair out of his eyes and grinned.

"Yeah, but he would have one thing we don't have. He has a gun," I mumbled right as everyone went silent. They all looked at me like they wanted me to continue. "The only reason any of us are even scared of this guy is because he has a gun. We're not scared of a plain stranger. It's the gun. You can run from a knife, but running from a gun is hopeless."

"Alright!" my teacher shouted as loudly as she could to mute us. "We are *not* talking about this *anymore*. The rules are that we hide in the corner, so that's what we are going to do. If *anyone* tries to do something differently, you will be sent to the principal's office. End of story." She huffed in anger and started her lesson. Her voice wobbled. I think she was shaking in fear, too.

- Emanuel AME Church, Charleston, June 17, 2015 -

I wasn't in town when the Emanuel AME Church shooting happened. I wasn't even in the country. The previous Christmas, my Grandma and Grandpa had one major gift for the entire family: a weeklong vacation on a Disney cruise through the Caribbean in June. It was supposed to be the happiest week of our lives. Little did we know that a heart-shattering tragedy occurred while we were away.

I remember sitting in the back seat of my mom's car as we left the cruise port on our way home; I always sit behind my dad, who always drives. Diagonal up from me, my mom pulled out her phone when she received a call from my Aunt Debbie. As she answered, she realized she had a few dozen missed texts from the week, since we had no signal on the boat. Aunt Debbie's voice rang through the phone, but it wasn't on speaker, so nobody else could hear her.

"Hello?" my mom said into the phone, then waited as Aunt Debbie spoke for a moment. "What funerals?" Pause. "What happened?" Another pause. "*What?*" She seemed frozen, the threads of her cloth seat coming undone and prying into her skin, sewing her in place. All she could do when my dad asked what happened was put her sister's call on speaker. "Say it again."

"*Did you hear? There was a mass shooting at the Mother Emanuel AME Church on Wednesday.*" She was breathless, like the words were constricting her airway.

"Emanuel AME? As in Charleston?" my dad asked, slowing the car as his heart rate increased. "The one in Charleston?"

I quickly became frightened and confused by the sound of my city's name. I didn't know what or where the church was, but I knew what a shooting was, and that was enough to scare me.

"*Yes. Downtown on Calhoun. Nine people died. They caught the man who did it in North Carolina the next day.*" Aunt Debbie paused to collect herself.

"What were the victims' names?" My dad questioned as he slowly took the next exit that appeared on the interstate, and my little sister and I looked at each other in confusion, not fully understanding what this meant; I was thirteen, and she was eight.

"I don't know all of them, but Senator Pinckney was one of them," she answered.

I finally realized what was happening, and my curiosity and devastation took over. "I'll look it up," I announced.

Pulling my iPhone 4 from my pocket, I opened Google and typed the letter "C," and the very first suggested result was "Charleston Church Shooting." I clicked the first link with shaky fingers and scrolled through the *Wikipedia* article. Once we parked in a gas station parking lot, I read off the names. Never once in my life had I ever seen my parents so saddened by an event that wasn't a family death, though this sure did feel like one. My dad, elbow on the car door frame beside the window, held his face in his hand. My mom covered her mouth with her hand as well, still holding her phone up with Aunt Debbie on the line.

"I'm sorry I had to be the one to deliver the message. I didn't think about how you guys might not have seen the news," Aunt Debbie mumbled.

I was barely old enough to understand that this was a race crime, an attack from a terrorist. But this was my hometown, a place full of love and unity and hope. I couldn't imagine how someone could do such a thing in a church, in the Holy City. This was my home. And now that such a thing happened so close to home, I took this attack personally. There was a unity walk across the Arthur Ravenel Bridge the day after we arrived home, and the moment I heard about it, I knew I needed to go, needed to support my friends and family of Charleston. My city felt different from that point forward. It felt stronger, a new bond.

- San Bernardino, California, December 2, 2015 -
- Hesston and Newton, Kansas, February 25, 2016 -
- Pulse Nightclub, Orlando, June 12, 2016 -
- Dallas Police, Texas, July 7, 2016 -
- Cincinnati Nightclub, Ohio, March 26, 2017 -
- Little Rock Nightclub, Arkansas, July 1, 2017 -
- Las Vegas, October 1, 2017 -
- Sutherland Springs, Texas, November 5, 2017 -
- Rancho Tehama Reserve, California, November 13, 2017 -
- Marshall County High School, Kentucky, January 28, 2018 -
- MSD High School, Florida, February 14, 2018 -
- Santa Fe High School, Texas, May 18, 2018 -
- Art All Night, Trenton, New Jersey, June 17, 2018 -
- Jacksonville Landing, Florida, August 26, 2018 -
- Florence Police, South Carolina, October 3, 2018 -
- Pittsburgh Synagogue, October 27, 2018 -
- Thousand Oaks, California, November 7, 2018 -
- Aurora, Illinois, February 15, 2019 -
- Virginia Beach, Virginia, May 31, 2019 -
- Gilroy Garlic Festival, California, July 28, 2019 -
- El Paso Walmart, Texas, August 3, 2019 -
- Dayton, Ohio, August 4, 2019 -
- Midland-Odessa, Texas, August 31, 2019 -
- Nevada Air Station, Florida, December 6, 2019 -
- And Every Shooting In Between -

A few months ago, in the morning at my school, I heard a sound from the hallway that, at first, I thought was a gunshot. Looking back, it only could've been a textbook falling, but in that moment, I was terrified. Even so, I imagined myself quickly – but shakily – standing from my seat and taking charge of the situation, a designated leader, as I've had more training for situations like this than anyone else in the room. With everyone's attention falling on me, I would usher them into the teacher's office silently and swiftly. Once everyone hid, I would barricade us in the room, shoving tables and bookshelves against the door. I would be ready – to fight or to die? I wasn't sure. But for whatever would come, I'd been preparing for it my entire life.

Every Monday, I attend a police class that serves as training for police-related events and scenarios, such as domestic violence, traffic stops, bank robberies, crisis negotiation, and active shooters. I know how to fight with objects around me if a shooter enters the room, because my goal is to eliminate the threat, to stop the killing and stop the dying, formulate a plan, a tactic for survival. Enough training and experience in fighting while the gunshots ring through a building has taught me that playing hide and seek with a shooter is not the way to survive. Sometimes the best thing to do is not to be a sitting duck in the corner of a room, but rather to just get the hell out of there – stay alive.

In February, 2018, there was a devastating school shooting at Marjory Stoneman Douglas High School in Parkland, Florida. After hearing about it enough on the news and the internet, I dreamt that there was a school shooting at my school. Such events were so common in the news and America in general that I can't help but imagine it frequently enough. But this dream felt so real, so terrifying, so life-threatening.

In my dream, the day began as normal, me rushing to brush my hair following my morning shower and sniffing two different perfume scents to determine which one smelled nicer today. My room appeared to have many of my decorations from when I was still in elementary school – innocent.

The scenery in this dream flashed to a school setting that was not my own, but it was mine in my dream. The hallway stretched long, with additional hallways off on each side, a maze that I would not be able to navigate. The lockers and walls were painted a solemn blue.

In the hall, a boy in all black passed by me, hood over his head, and his arm rammed into my shoulder, causing me to stumble back. I stared at the boy's back as he continued past me. He reminded me of a kid who used to go to school there last year. Not someone I knew in real life, but myself in my dream recognized him, disliked him.

"Idiot," I muttered under my breath.

Like in a movie, everything fast-forwarded to a later class in the day, just a few moments before my teacher would pass out a quiz. The teacher was one of the male teachers I've had before in real life, one who advocated for better safety precautions in school a couple years before. Everyone had their heads down, reading over their notes as quickly as possible, when the loudest noise erupted from the hall. Everyone immediately knew what it was and how to react: by screaming. The sound rang again, several times throughout the hall, like a textbook repeatedly falling, or a cascade of fireworks whizzing past. In the hall, children shrieked until the next loud noise silenced them.

In slow motion, the class rose from their seats and sprinted toward the wall, ducking and dragging other students with them as they clambered over desks and chairs. The teacher moved faster than I'd ever seen as he locked the door without standing directly in front of it. With the help of a boy in the class, he shoved some filing cabinets in front of the door. The doorway is considered the *fatal funnel*, nothing but a thin wood surface and glass for a metal bullet to pierce through, all the way into the room until a body catches it.

The memory of this nightmare comes in flashes. I imagined a war-zone as someone shoved me onto the floor, cupping their hand over my mouth, which busted my lip. I hadn't realized I had been crying until now, loud sobs slipping out of my mouth between my lips like water from a faucet or hair through fingers. Why had I not awakened myself yet? I quickly collected myself. Suddenly not caring for personal space, I helped silence people, hands over their mouths to muffle their screams and cries. The lights turned off so dark that all I could see was people's wide eyes and reflective tears. Everyone froze as the gunshots ceased. I assumed the last one had been the school's resource officer taking him out. But I was wrong because a second later, the shooter cursed and dropped something that I believed was a magazine, which he replenished and began firing again. He came prepared. Determined. And I knew it was the guy from the hallway encounter that morning.

The nightmare flashed to show that my teacher joined us on the floor. He pulled his phone out of his pocket and dialed 9-1-1 as he checked to make sure none of us were in sight of the door. In a nation so traumatized by mass shootings, I was beyond grateful for my teacher's ability to function under all of this stress.

"H-hello. There's a school shooter." He told the operator.

The shooter jiggled the handle of the door. Everyone's eyes locked on the door. The filing cabinet kept the shooter out, but he still shot at the cabinet.

I don't remember exactly what happened next in this nightmare, but some students were shot, and I held pressure on their wounds, kept them alive as long as I could. Everything felt so realistic that I could remember the feeling of warm, red liquid seeping between my fingers, of the rise and fall of their chests as someone performed CPR, of the shrieks ringing in my ears. Once I finally took charge, ordering students to sneak out the windows as low to the ground as they could possibly run, I saved every student in that room except for most of the ones who were shot; there weren't enough tissues to plug bullet holes. I tried my hardest.

If this ever happened in real life, I'd like to think I could truly take charge like that, but quicker. I'd like to think I'd be ready to fight, to run in a randomized zig-zag to destroy the shooter's aim, to save every person around me as fearful adrenaline pushed me through the entire event.

In the past few years, I have discovered that I am fearful of simply walking around downtown. It isn't just dark alleyways. It's school, struggling to catch my breath when an administrator comes over the intercom in the classrooms to tell us we're in a lockdown. It's in the churches, synagogues, streets, clubs, movie theaters, concerts, restaurants, malls, backyards, parking lots, traffic stops, and grocery stores. I should still think fireworks and gunshots sound the same, but I know they don't. I fear the dark, even in my own house. Not because there might be a goblin under the couch or a suspicious car on the street, but because there might be a shooter on my porch or lingering in the shadows.

When I was younger, I used to not care if I died. You could've called me suicidal if you wanted to, but that's not me anymore. I want to live now, want to grow old with a spouse and kids and have a career I've always dreamed of, and it infuriates me and terrifies me that someone else could, in an instance, take a life, just end it in the time it takes from the pulled trigger to send a bullet into a chest. Not just mine, but anybody's. I want to die on my own time, not at the hands of a murderer. That is my worst fear. And that is America.

Panacea

Panacea

Panacea

Panacea

Panacea

Judgment

My Aunt Debbie tucked me into the pink-blanketed daybed and kissed my forehead. She ignored each of my complaints about not wanting to sleep, about wanting to stay up late with her to talk with the adults. After sliding open the window, she cooed for me to sleep because the sooner I drifted off, the sooner we could have our next adventure. Nodding and closing my eyes, I waited for her to shut the door and for her distant footsteps on the stairs to echo into silence. I tried to fall asleep to the sound of the rushing creek and hushed voices whispering about grown-up things over wine and beer at the kitchen table.

When I closed my eyes, I pictured the creek out back. The water gently rushing over the rocks. The soothing whoosh and drip-drip of the water splashing against itself and the side of the creek and the rocks. Fish rarely swam in it, but I wondered what it would be like to be a fish in the creek. I wanted to be a minnow because they were small and fast. If I were a minnow, I could swim over the pebbles and between the bright green plants. My face would cool in the refreshing water, the pressure and temperature so calming. Perhaps it would feel like the ocean back home in Charleston, except not as salty, so probably more like my grandma's pool.

Following the creek's path, I could venture all the way down the mountain and find my way to the big lake that told me I was in Maggie Valley, a place so beautiful it could be mythical, yet still just a small town thirty-six miles from Asheville, North Carolina. The town was quaint, nestled in a valley full of lively green trees, vibrant flowers and leaves, and a thirty-foot-wide creek paralleling the main road. I would already know my way to the lake as a minnow. And I could lead my new fish friends there because I was good at making friends. I dreamt a lot – of being a fish. Then, the next morning came sooner, just like Aunt Debbie said.

The next morning, when I woke up, I tiptoed past Mommy and Daddy, both of whom were still sleeping, and raced into Aunt Debbie's room, telling her it was time to go sit on the porch swing and watch the sun come up.

Groaning, she slowly crept out of bed and followed me. Her new dog, Bailey, snuck out with us, her collar jingling loudly with each step. She was too scared to jump onto the swing with me and Aunt Debbie, so she settled onto the porch and watched the birds fluttering away from their nests for the morning's meal.

My feet rocked back and forth under the porch swing as I tried to help push us. Aunt Debbie did all of the work, though, propelling us backwards with her feet with enough momentum to keep us moving for a few minutes.

"How'd you sleep?" she asked, softly to not wake up Grandpy, whose bedroom was through the window beside the swing.

I smiled. "Good."

She nodded and put her arm around me. "Good. Me, too."

I put my finger over my lip. "We have to be quiet so the hummingbirds will come to the feeder."

"Oh, right. Very quiet." She put her finger over her lip, too, then stared out at the yard for any hummingbirds or chipmunks that strolled through.

After a few minutes of waiting and trying to be extremely still on the swing, we saw a green hummingbird approach. The bird looked young, but it had already mastered the art of being able to fly in one place without moving. It sipped from the red sugar-water feeder that hung from the ceiling of the porch. A blue hummingbird came a short while later, and after some sort of bird conversation, the green bird left.

A squirrel pranced across the yard, and Bailey barked at it. Aunt Debbie quickly shushed her and held her back before she could run after the squirrel. When I looked back up at the hummingbird feeder, the bird had left, probably because of Bailey. There was a knock on the window beside me, and I jumped at the sight of my Grandpy's face in the window. (Grandpy was Aunt Debbie's and my mom's Daddy.) He laughed and waved at me. Excited to see that he was awake, I jumped off of the swing, nearly landing on Bailey, and rushed inside.

After we got ready, Aunt Debbie took me down to the town. Normally my mom went with me, but she was very pregnant, and my dad had to stay at the house to help take care of her. We walked around some shops. Most were full of souvenirs, since it seemed like there were more tourists and people passing through in a year than people who actually lived there.

We wandered into a store that had a lot of clothes and knickknacks like pocket knives and keychains and toy guns and little cups Aunt Debbie told me were called shot glasses. Each of the shirts had designs or slogans I didn't understand or couldn't read yet, since I was only four. Tons of colorful flags lined the walls, including the one that I recognized as the American flag. There was another red, white, and blue flag, but it was different and had the shape of an X on it. An entire wall was lined with guns that were a lot bigger than the one Daddy had on his police belt.

Once I found the section with the keychains, I fumbled through them in search of one with my name on it. Mine was always hard to find because Mommy said it was the original spelling, and a lot of people didn't spell it that way anymore. She said it made me unique. I just thought it was annoying. But I found a solar powered light-up keychain with my name on it, and Aunt Debbie let me get it, since it was so rare to find one with my name. But then she directed me away from the flags and shirts and keychains, over to a section with kids' toys and stuffed animals. It was weird that she didn't want me spending too much time looking at the things on the walls, but I didn't say anything.

"Pick whatever you want, Honey," she said, nudging me with her hand. I pointed to a picture frame on a shelf, which seemed to confuse her because it wasn't a toy. In the frame was a picture of Hilary Duff, the girl who played Lizzie on the *Disney Channel* show, *Lizzie McGuire*. She was my favorite actress on my favorite show.

She raised an eyebrow. "Why do you want that?"

"I like her."

Nodding in understanding, she slowly led me away from the frames. "She's very pretty, Honey, but that's not a toy. You'd have to put an actual picture in that. Come pick a toy."

None of the toys were particularly my *favorite*, so I roamed over to the stuffed animals section and found a small pig that Aunt Debbie and I both thought was perfect. We left the store shortly thereafter with the keychain and the small stuffed pig that I named *Maggie*.

As we walked on the porch outside of the long strip of shops back to the car, the wind blew, giving an unexpected coolness to the hot summer air. The leaves on the trees and the flowers planted in front of the porch danced in the breeze. It felt like the most secure, pleasant, mythical place in the world, protected by mountains. An oasis.

+ + +

Twelve years later, on one of my biannual trips to Maggie Valley, I began to look at the town through a new lens. Having learned about the Civil War in at least five different grades in school already, as well as growing up in Charleston, I knew the difference between racial equality and racial tolerance. I became very aware of racism, sexism, homophobia, and transphobia through the years.

On the car drive up to Maggie Valley, I noticed several signs that illustrated the silhouettes of a man and a woman from restroom placards with a plus sign in the middle, an equal sign after, and the words "TRADITIONAL MARRIAGE" written after. The sign seemed like a math equation, like no other variables could exist. It infuriated me, but I convinced myself it was just the rural areas, that Maggie Valley would continue to be the calming oasis it had been for me as a child.

With my mother and little sister, who was nearly twelve years old, I walked through the same shop where I had gotten the flashing name keychain and stuffed pig, both of which I still had. The entire shop caused me to wince. Now, I recognized the flags hanging on the wall as Confederate Army flags. The guns that had once hung on the wall, some of them considered military grade, now sat behind glass in a case at the counter, like jewelry. The Marjory Stoneman Douglas school shooting in Parkland, Florida, happened only six months before this, and the Emanuel Church Shooting in my hometown had only been three years before. I nearly gagged at how easily accessible the guns were.

Some shirts on display had cruel remarks about police officers and other first responders, which particularly offended me because of my father's occupation. One shirt had a design of a scruffy-looking guy smiling with a finger over his lips as if to say "shh," while his other hand dropped a small pill into a wine glass. I knew exactly what it was referring to. Another design caught my eye because of the rainbow, but once I read it, I immediately felt ill, wishing the floor beneath me would collapse so I could escape, maybe dig my way to the creek and pretend to be a fish again, breathe in the water instead of the toxic air around me. The shirt said, "Kill the Homosexuals." Behind it was a shirt that insinuated the only true purpose for lesbians was for the pleasure of men. A shirt in low quantity, indicating that it was very popular, read, "White and Proud." A few feet over, I saw a man eyeing a "Come and Take It" shirt with an military-grade rifle on it, like he was prepared to purchase it.

Every now and then, I came across a funny shirt, like one that read, "I'm with stupid," and a matching one that read, "I'm stupid." But no number of funny shirts could ever balance out the sickening ones. I found candy and a bracelet for my friend and exited the store, even though my mother and sister were still inside looking at bumper stickers and pens with names on them.

I sat on a bench on the porch outside the strip of stores. A group of girls waltzed past me and into the store with the shirts. Resisting the urge to warn them was difficult, but I remained silent, staring through the flowers, which had grown quite tall, out at the mountain view.

Panacea

A man in a red pickup truck parked in an open space near me and looked at me as he clambered out of his truck. He wore a red flannel shirt, dirty jeans, a cowboy hat, and cowboy boots. His pale white skin almost reflected sunlight at me. His eyes looked me up and down, but when he noticed my gaze, he looked away, turning his head in another direction as he shut the door of his pickup. A Confederate flag was printed on the side of his hat. I wondered about the family he would go home to. If he would buy a little stuffed animal for his young daughter for her to name *Maggie*. If his wife knew how he looked at other women when she wasn't with him. If he ever worried about his daughter getting shot at school or simply even by her Daddy's gun that he accidentally forgot to properly lock up one day. If his daughter was taught to fear or hate people who aren't white. If he was proud of that.

As I waited for my mother and sister to come outside to the bench where I was sitting, I recalled all the people I had ever seen in this town. Very few people were children, and most of the children or teenagers I saw were tourists who were staying in houses by the lake for a church retreat. Most people were older – even the ones working at the *Bojangle's* fast food restaurant up the road or the gas station across the street. Nearly everyone, if not every single person in the town, was white, except for one or two Native

American families that didn't live up the road in Cherokee. And I knew that, in this town, the Confederate flags were not for heritage, but rather for racism itself. Such a place made me miss Charleston, where the racists were fewer and farther between, and the activists were more abundant. A place where I felt free to be myself, rather than having to put up a façade.

My mother and sister left the store with a small bag of candies and unnecessary knick-knacks. I asked my mom if we could leave, go over to the park up the road. People were almost never at that park, even though it had a huge grassy field, a large play area for kids, a basketball court, and a running track. With the time of day, we could even see the sun setting behind the mountain, glowing orange like smeared paint across the sky. Noticing my anxiety and discomfort, she agreed to take us where almost no people were.

I sat in the field, even though I was allergic to it. In the breeze, the grass blades blew against my skin, tickling and creating an almost-burning-sensation of anaphylaxis. It felt rather satisfying, lying in the grass and admiring the view of the mountains and wispy clouds in the sky. My hair flicked across my face, and I closed my eyes. The sun barely peeked over the mountains as though to say "Goodnight." No voices echoed in the valley's park other than that of my sister, who laughed as she slid down the slide that everyone except her knew she was too big for.

"Come play with me," she called out, waving over at me once she reached the bottom of the slide.

Giggling at her childishness, I shook my head and stared over at the road, watching cars pass by. My mother sat in her car and read a new book on her Kindle. I heard my sister attempting to climb up the slide, even though I had told her she couldn't. When she fell down to the bottom, she shouted, "I'm okay!" to us, then ran over to the swings, as if it was the most natural thing to do.

If I closed my eyes long enough to focus on the sounds around me, I could almost hear the creek, which was across the road. When the wind blew the grass against me, it felt like I was being blown, too, floating through the air to the creek, and maybe if I swam through the creek, like a minnow, long enough, I could find the ocean, and I could swim home.

But the wind stopped, and I couldn't hear the creek. Each car that passed, I knew, could have carried another racist, another man wearing an anti-black shirt, preaching his opinion on women's bodies as though anyone were listening, carrying a loaded shotgun in case he encountered someone who wasn't white or straight, and, yet, each person in each car was still a human being. Living around people who believed a person's worth was determined by the color of their skin, the gender of the person they love, or the sex they were born with were thoughts that terrified me. But I loved the beauty of the place itself – the mountain views and whooshing creek and clean air. So, I stared up at the clouds that turned pink in the sunset up above and pretended that nobody else existed.

Panacea

Panacea

Panacea

Panacea

Panacea

From Charleston to Parkland

As much as I sometimes dislike living in Charleston, South Carolina, it will always be a part of who I am, especially after the Mother Emanuel AME Church Shooting only a dozen miles from my house. I wasn't in town when the shooting happened, but if I had been, I probably would've heard sirens from ambulances and police cars. Ever since I was four, I've been able to distinguish what sirens come from which type of vehicle, like they were voices from people I know. A crime scene investigator lives across the highway from me, and I assume she would have been sent to such an emergency. My father, a sergeant in the police department, would've gone, too. He knew a few of the victims.

At only thirteen years old, I felt as though I could do absolutely nothing to make a difference, silenced by the acidic taste of age doused my skin. Because in this time, I'm the powerless child, and there was an evil man with a powerful gun, and all the powerful adults around me didn't know what to do about him.

My best friend told me about a unity walk across the biggest bridge in the state, and so I went because, with all the hate and sorrow bottled in each person's body in Charleston, we needed some sort of unity, a time to reflect and absorb and breathe together as one city, one body. Organizers wanted at least fifteen hundred participants, but they ended up with over ten thousand. I walked hand in hand with my best friend, while holding a poster that read: "Charleston Strong." I walked between my friend, her brother, and an African American woman that I had never met before. The woman told me that she and her mother attended the church and chose not to go that day, and that the simple decision of staying home, flipping through television channels and eating microwaved dinners on their couch, saved their lives. The entire way up the cable bridge, the woman sang songs, most of which were hymnals, but she sang one or two others, which I didn't recognize. Her vigorous voice singing "Amazing Grace" at the top of the bridge, when everyone stopped to hold hands and pray and have a moment of silence, encouraged everyone else to present their own voices. All of the cars that passed by us slowed down from their normal sixty miles per hour to forty or thirty, and some even slowed down to twenty. They gave acknowledgment and respect as they waved and honked their car horns. Chills snaked up my spine as I sang with ten thousand strangers, and I knew that this unity was what my city needed even more of.

After that day, in search of how to unify the community, I decided to write a card to the members of the church to show my love and support for them. But why have one card when I could have many? With permission of the mall owner, I set up two tables in the middle of the mall where children and adults could craft a card of their own, whether it be a loving drawing or a heartfelt letter. Freedom of art and expression. After two days of standing at the table, rocking back and forth on my calloused feet while talking to families who all had stories or opinions to share, I collected one hundred ninety cards and delivered them to the church, specifically to a family member of Sharonda Coleman-Singleton, who was a victim of the shooting. The woman wore all black, and mascara marks traced down her cheeks. She hugged me, engulfing me in thanks and the scent of candles and flowers, and said she had to go back into the church for a service.

My family and I took ten minutes to leave after that. We stood in front of the tall white church, following the perimeter of the property with our eyes. Police officers blocked the entire road with barricades. It smelled slightly less of car exhaust than I expected, which was partially because of the lack of cars, but it was mostly because of hundreds of flowers leaned up against the fence with candles in front. The fence was barely visible, with all the bouquets and crosses and posters and balloons. Color sprouted in front of the white church and black fence. Turned a situation of black and white to a rainbow of nurture.

I had to give something. Any possible comfort or support I could give them. And this would have to do for now.

By the time February fourteenth, 2018, came around, when a school shooting occurred at Marjory Stoneman Douglas High School in Parkland, Florida, mass shootings were a part of the daily news. Nobody wanted to become insensitive to it because every mass shooting is important to talk about. But the human brain fails to treat every emotional trauma the same when the trauma is repeated so frequently. Even so, all mass shootings always hit close to home for me after the church shooting, and I have an impulsive need to call attention to the situation and help a fellow suffering, devastated community.

I've never gone into anaphylactic shock, but with my allergies, I've been extremely close to it. Not being able to help the suffering families all over the world when people are killed, especially by guns, feels like anaphylaxis. Dizzy and nauseous, like I'm spinning and spinning and spinning. Tight throat, trouble breathing, quick heartbeat, anxiety building and pooling and overflowing. Shook me in shudders until my ribs were sore and my lungs were singed.

One of my best friends lives fifteen minutes from Stoneman Douglas, and her school was only five minutes away. I laid awake for a few nights after the shooting, wracked with the idea that it could've been her school, due to the close proximity and my way of falling to the worst case scenario whenever given the opportunity. While I have had training for how to handle active shooter situations, she had not. At least, not other than lockdown drills. My stomach panged at the thought of a gunman trudging through her school, her huddled under a desk with people she barely knew after just recently starting a new semester, her whole body vibrating in an a panic attack, traumatized as she texted her mother: "Tengo miedo. Te amo." *I'm scared. I love you.* Spelling errors from her petite body rattling. She'd be okay, but she'd be silent for days, flinching at every footstep, every door closing, every loud breath, every school classroom or hallway. Terrified in the fetal position.

Like I had done for the Charleston Church Shooting, I decided to make cards for the Parkland School Shooting a month after it happened. In the beginning of April of that year, a little less than two months since the school shooting, I'd be going to visit my friend in Florida, so I'd be close enough to the school to hand-deliver the cards, as I had done with the church shooting. I figured I'd get a lot of cards at the mall, but it seemed as though so many shootings had happened between the day of the shooting and the days I stood at the mall for eight hours. After two days at the mall, I only received a few dozen cards, so I advertised at my school as well, finally totaling at two hundred six cards.

The morning that my family and I were leaving Florida to come home was the morning we delivered the cards. I had read every single one, a few paper cuts on my fingers like stray pencil marks on a sketch artist's paper. Any cards that appeared too insensitive were removed because this was to spread comfort and the feeling of community understanding from one grief-stricken place to another. Parkland had not had a unity walk like Charleston, so I needed to help provide a sense of unity in one of the only ways I knew how from such a far distance.

I could hardly breathe the entire car ride to the school from the hotel. In the back seat of the car, my body temperature rose, turning my hands clammy. My head pulsed in time with my heartbeat, faster and faster as the distance between me and the school grew smaller. The air felt different when I rolled my window down and let my hand dance. Quiet. Empty.

Worst case scenario. I imagined us pulling up to the gate of the school, being told we could not deliver the cards and support because it was a random box full of unknown papers. They'd ask me to step out of my car, and they'd search me for weapons, find nothing, and then continue to prevent me from entering the campus. And they'd have every right to do so because trauma creates paranoia. I just wanted to help bridge understanding and empathy from two communities.

We pulled up to a stop light in the lane to turn left. In my lap sat the box of cards, and my entire body paused at the sight of a sign that read, "Marjory Stoneman Douglas High School," with an arrow pointing to the left, and it felt all too real. I'd never been in a school with a gunman, never experienced a real shooting, but I knew I was about to see many, many people who had.

Planted trees lined the road to the school, and there were seventeen of them with red bows around the middle of their trunks. One for each victim. But as soon as I saw the fence around the school, posters strapped to the metal diamonds with the fence almost completely covered, my breathing came out choked, suffocated. After showing the police officer at the gate my father's ID and police badge, as well as my box of cards, they let us in, and I whimpered softly to myself as we searched for a parking spot, staring down at my box instead of the school, as though I would see deep bullet holes in the exterior of the building.

I had to take a moment for myself as I exited the car, collecting my breaths and tears in time to enter the school with the box. As I handed the box to the woman at the desk, explaining that I had come all the way from Charleston, South Carolina, to give support, she thanked me. A boy wearing a "#MSDStrong" shirt passed by, as we had arrived when classes changed, and it was the most silent class change I had ever heard. The quiet was deafening. But it was the most symbolic, important silence. I hadn't expected anything else.

Panacea

Panacea

Panacea

Panacea

Panacea

Grandpy's New Eulogy

Dear Grandpy,

I haven't seen you in person since April 28th, 2016, and it pains me to say that I've started to forget how you look. I can recognize you in pictures, but it's hard to imagine you otherwise. It makes me wish I had more pictures with you, more memories. I often wonder what new memories we could've made together if you were still here. If we could've gone to California together to visit your sister, or to Texas to visit your cousin. If we could've visited a college together, maybe show you where I'll go to school when I graduate high school. If you could've taught me how to build things, like a chair or a desk. If you could've shown me how to drive. If we could've sat on the back porch of the Maggie

Valley house to watch the water rushing in the creek down below. If you could've read my first book.

We stopped really doing things together when I was around seven or so. You started getting older and sicker, exhausted from the long life you'd been living. And I was growing up, too busy for the short drive to your house to see you, even after you moved to Charleston to live with Aunt Debbie. I regret that.

I remember we used to watch movies together. You watched movies differently than anyone else I'd ever seen: you kept your eyes closed and let your mouth hang open. Before you could even hit the *Play* button, you fell asleep. Every single time. Aunt Debbie and I would joke that we could put in a movie you wanted to watch, take it out when you fell asleep, and put in a girly movie, so we could tease you afterwards. You slept through a couple Barbie movies, Grandpy. You slept through me playing with horse toys on the floor of the living room. The horses were too small for Barbies, but sometimes I'd place them on the horse and have them ride around into the small, wooden stables anyway. I specifically remember one horse – a small foal, brown in color and white legs from the knees down – had a broken leg. He was the only horse I can still remember the name of because you and Aunt Debbie found some tape and a small piece of wood that just so happened to be the perfect fit to give this amputee horse a prosthetic. We called him Peg, and he could trot around again, good as new. Sometimes I would play with these toys as we watched *Flicka* or *The Black Beauty* on the television, which were two of my favorite horse movies. I'm not a horse girl anymore, but I have appreciation for that time in my life anyway because you were there.

I go to Aunt Debbie's a lot nowadays. I visit with her and her husband Tony and her dog Bailey, who isn't doing too well, always walking in circles and forgetting where she is. Bailey doesn't know how to act since you passed away. Honestly, none of us do, even four years later. But I think of you all the time. Especially at Aunt Debbie's, when I sit at the kitchen table instead of the automatic recliner; I can't bring myself to sit in something that only *you* were supposed to sit in.

Perhaps I have a thing for tributes. I want to keep the chair empty as a tribute for you. In fact, I almost feel offended when people sit in that chair because it's yours. Whenever someone enters your bedroom, I prefer to hang back in the doorway, taking in the deep shade of grey-ish blue and attempting to prevent myself from sneezing over the dust particles wisping about in the air. I'm scared I'm not supposed to be there, so I never spend long in your room. I don't know if it is out of respect or out of the pain of missing you.

Around the time that you passed away, I was diagnosed with anxiety and depression. It landed me in the nurse's office at school every single day, and sometimes I needed to sort paperclips by color. I think I needed to control something. The world felt like it was crippling around me as I was losing a best friend. I had no control over the fact that you were leaving me, that you felt ready to move on. This anxiety granted me one of my biggest regrets.

When you were in the rehab center, I was too anxious to handle sitting in a chair at your bedside. My whole family visited you every day after school and work, and after twenty minutes of watching you sleep or channel surf or refuse to eat your dinner, I sat in the car in the parking lot. Sometimes, I pretended I was driving the car because that was something I could control. And sometimes I just cried. Everyone always talks about the stages of grief, but nobody talks about the anxiety and depressive anticipation in the time leading up to an expected death, how the world feels like it won't move fast or slow enough, how all hope dissipates every morning when you remember that someone you love is dying.

I remember the last day I had hope about you getting better. It was roughly two weeks before you passed away, and we were talking about sea animals. You told me you liked sea turtles, and I mentioned that we could go to the aquarium to see them. You shocked me when you said you had never been to the aquarium. I used to go all the time with my other grandparents, them watching as I slipped my small hands into the touch-tank and squealed from excitement at holding a starfish. The thought of you missing out on such an engaging experience saddened me.

"Grandpy, you need to get better," I told you as I shoveled a spoon into some sherbet for you to eat.

You shrugged, like I was encouraging you to eat a carrot.

"I want you to get better, so we can go to the aquarium together. You just have to get your strength back, and then we can go and see the turtles and penguins and stingrays. Please try to get better, so we can do that," I egged on, pouting out my bottom lip.

With a sigh, you nodded. "Okay, I'll try."

I smiled. "Yay! Now, eat this." I fed you a bite of the sherbet, to which you gave no resistance to for the first time in a week; I was almost always the only one who could get you to eat.

I prided myself on this. Later that night, though, my parents warned me that you probably wouldn't get better, but with hope, I assured them that making a list of things we could do when you left the rehab would motivate your recovery. I planned that every day I would add to the list of what we could do. But the very next day, the doctors announced that you only had a few weeks left with us. Two weeks later, you were gone.

There's a lot of regrets in my thoughts, but not spending more time with you while you were healthy is one of the biggest ones, almost as big as not pushing you enough to get healthy again when you started taking a turn. I'd give anything to watch a movie with you again, to shop at Ingles for Moose Tracks ice cream and apple fritters while Aunt Debbie bought healthier items, to bring you a homemade slushy for you to drink on Aunt Debbie's back porch with us during our break from gardening, to play a game of cards, to open gifts on Christmas Eve morning and see whatever Aunt Debbie picked out to put your name on. I'd give anything to see my best friend again. I miss you, and I love you.

Your first granddaughter,
Caitlin

Panacea

Panacea

Panacea

Panacea

Acknowledgements

To Mom and Dad, thank you. You always listened to my dreams, my hopes for the future, my passions for change in such a twisted world. When I told you that I wanted to be a writer, you didn't question my sanity, just handed me a pencil and let me have at it. Seven years later, I am publishing my first book, and I am eternally grateful for your support. You both taught me to be a kid and a grown up at the same time. I owe my maturity, my experiences, my love, and my life to you. Mom, thank you for constantly listening and for fighting for me. And Dad, thank you for making it to almost all of my readings, despite your crazy jobs, and thank you for your work on my cover. I love you both. This never would've been possible without you.

To Emily, my sister, thank you. Thank you for humoring me when we'd play teacher and student in our old playroom. Thank you for letting me create crazy stories with Barbies and toy cars and shadow puppets. Thank you for sitting on the floor of my room and listening to me read a story I wrote. Thank you for not tattling when you knew I was up late reading or writing by flashlight. Thank you for realizing your own potential as a writer. Thank you for writing with me.

To my creative writing teachers and second parents, Mr. F. Rutledge Hammes, Ms. Danielle DeTiberus, Mrs. Beth Webb Hart, Mr. Sean Scapelleto, and Mrs. Rene Miles, thank you. I always wanted to write, but you are the ones who taught me how. You taught me to enjoy writing and to enjoy life. Thank you for encouraging me to live better, to write better, and to live a life worth writing about. No words will ever express how grateful I am for the support you have all given me since I was an obnoxious sixth grader who accidentally named a character *James Potter*, completely unaware of my mistake. Now, I'm an obnoxious eighteen-year-old, but I have grown, I've learned, I've lived, I've laughed, and I've loved, and I'll never stop doing all of those things. Mrs. Miles, thank you for reading *The Polar Express* to us and giving us bells to jingle to show we believed. Mr. Scapelleto, thank you for teaching me the importance of sounds and of having fun. Ms. DeTiberus, thank you for helping me during the hardest mental health time period of my life and for always offering a laugh to spread or an ear to listen. Mrs. Hart, thank you for showing me how to be vulnerable in my nonfiction writing and for always checking in on us students every day after we lost one of our own, showing us grief is a long process we all experience. Mr. Hammes, thank you for always helping me become inspired and for always helping me work through the hard stuff, like applying to college and writing a book. Thank you all for the past seven years of my life.

To my friends and classmates, thank you. River, Alex, Maya Cline, Lou, Caroline, Katie, Julian, Maya Green, Loulou, Christina, and Layla, you've all been present in every single day of my life since sixth grade. You're all my best friends. We grew together, learned together, laughed together, loved together, grieved together, and made memories together. I can't imagine my life without all of you. No longer sitting in class with the eleven of you will be the most agonizing, excruciating transition. You're all so smart, with such beautiful, kind souls, and I will miss you all every single day. Thank you for keeping my secrets, for giving advice, for sticking together as a team. I will cherish you all forever. Thank you to all the students who were part of our class for any period of time: Gigi, Katie B., Jack, Ted, Clara, and Lucinda. I would also like to thank Alex Kuffel-Barbanel for joining our class for nearly two years, for always offering support, a laugh, an intellectual statement, an interesting story, and many memories. This class has grown so close together over the past few years, and I'm thankful for every single moment with all of you. Thank you for sharing a perfect coming-of-age moment in Lake Logan. Thank you for never having the type of drama that tears classes apart. I would also like to thank Madison, for always being a best friend since third grade, for the dinner dates in the *Cook-Out* parking lot, for inviting me to your tennis matches, for coming to my readings, and for continuing to be my best friend, even after you left school. And thank you Yvette, for coming into my life at just the right time, for the late-night conversations, for teaching me things I never even knew about myself, and for the art on the front cover. Thank you Mary Coastal for your art on the back cover and for always supporting everything I do. You guys always supported me over the years as wonderful friends, and I wouldn't be the same without you guys. Thank you to all of my friends who were always there when I needed them and who could listen to my rants, my heartbreaks, and my ridiculous jokes. Thank you for helping me grow.

To my aunts, uncles, cousins, grandparents, and distant relatives, thank you. You all helped me become who I am, and you've always supported my passions. You've all been there for me through the ups and downs, the losses and gains, the happy and sad. Thank you to those of you who were able to come to my readings. Thank you for giving me a life worth writing about, especially Aunt Debbie, Tony, Aunt Dawn, Grandpy, Grandma, and Grandpa. None of this would have been possible without all of you. Thank you.

To my mentor, Mrs. Cindi Carver-Futch, thank you for helping me through the writing and editing process of this book. It wouldn't have been possible without you.

To my tenth grade Algebra II Honors teacher, Mr. Lyons, thank you for all of your help with my Cards for Parkland project. It never would've been as successful as it was without you.

To my middle and high school nurses, thank you for helping me through my anxiety and other health problems over the years.

To my fourth-grade teacher, Mrs. Blalock, thank you. I didn't know I liked writing so much until you encouraged me to keep writing. I don't know who I would be if you didn't help me pursue my passion. Thank you.

To my preschool teachers, Miss Lexa and Miss Sarah, thank you. You will both always be monumental people in my life. Thank you for helping raise me in those first couple years of my life.

To my readers, thank you because a book cannot succeed without all of you.

Panacea

Panacea

Panacea

Panacea

Made in United States
Orlando, FL
19 December 2022